NOSTELL
PRIORY

Yorkshire

THE NATIONAL TRUST

Nostell Priory is on the A638 five miles south-east of Wakefield towards Doncaster.

Acknowledgements

This guide is heavily indebted to the previous edition written by Gervase Jackson-Stops and revised by Roger Carr-Whitworth. It has been written by Sophie Raikes, Research Assistant in the Yorkshire region, and by Tim Knox, the Trust's Architectural Historian. They gratefully acknowledge the help of the following for giving permission to reproduce works of art, drawings and photographs, and for providing information: Lord St Oswald, Mark Winn, Sir John Soane's Museum, London, Bodleian Library, Oxford, Mrs Irene Parnell, and Mr and Mrs Hubbard. We are also indebted to Janette Ray Associates, Chris Burnett Associates and Northern Archaeological Associates for their reports on the history of the park and garden and the 17th-century house; to Andrew Halstead, who indexed and transcribed many of the papers in the Nostell Archive; to Susan Stuart for her advice on the Gillows Archive; and to the Archivist of the West Yorkshire Archive Service and his staff. We would also like to thank the Heritage Lottery Fund (HLF), National Art Collections Fund, Victoria & Albert Museum Purchase Grant Fund, National Heritage Memorial Fund and the Friends of Nostell for their generous grant aid in purchasing chattels, buildings and land, and carrying out conservation and restoration projects.

(*Front cover*) Sir Rowland Winn, 5th Bt, and his wife Sabine beside the Chippendale desk in the Library, which was decorated for them by Robert Adam; by Hugh Douglas Hamilton (Library)

(*Title-page*) A two-handled Worcester cup, decorated with a view of the entrance front (Breakfast Room)

(*Back cover*) The Top Hall. Adam designed matching friezes for the doorcase and chimneypiece

CONTENTS

Plans of the House *inside front cover*

Introduction *page* 4

Tour of the House 6

The Interior 6

The Lower Hall 6

The South Staircase 8

The Top Hall 9

The Breakfast Room 12

The Crimson Room 15

The Bathrooms 17

The State Dressing Room 18

The State Bedroom 19

The State Dining Room 21

The Saloon 22

The Tapestry Room 26

The Library 28

The Billiard Room 31

The Drawing Room 32

The Little Dining Room 33

The North Staircase 35

The Muniments Room *page* 37

The Museum Room 37

The Servants' Hall 40

The Exterior 40

The Stables 42

The Park, Pleasure Grounds and Gardens 44

Nostell Priory and the Winns 49

The Medieval Priory 49

The 17th-century House 50

The 4th Baronet, Col. Moyser and James Paine 51

The 5th Baronet and Robert Adam 54

The 6th Baronet 58

John and Charles Winn 58

The 1st and 2nd Barons St Oswald 61

The 20th Century 62

Bibliography 64

Family Tree *inside back cover*

NOSTELL PRIORY

Nostell's most loved treasure is its 18th-century doll's-house. It is still miraculously complete with its original fittings – from the plate rack in the kitchen to the little mahogany chairs in the bedrooms. Nostell Priory itself has also triumphantly survived the threats of fire and mining subsidence, and remains a showpiece of Robert Adam's decorative genius. And the superb furniture of Thomas Chippendale, Britain's greatest cabinet-maker, still sits in the rooms for which it was made.

The house takes its name from the priory dedicated to St Oswald that was founded here in the 12th century. At the Dissolution of the Monasteries in the 1530s, the priory buildings were converted into a dwelling house, which was acquired in 1654 by the Winn family, who have lived here ever since.

Sir ROWLAND WINN, 4th BARONET, returned from the Grand Tour in 1729 and began to build the present house on a site slightly to the north of the old priory in about 1735 and lay out the parkland around it. A local gentleman-architect, Colonel James Moyser, provided plans, which were modified by the young James Paine. Paine was employed at Nostell for over 30 years from 1736 and was responsible for many of the interiors, including the two staircases, the State Bedroom and the State Dining Room, all of which retain Paine's rococo plasterwork.

When Sir ROWLAND WINN, 5th BARONET, inherited in 1765, he commissioned Robert Adam

The Adam ceiling in the Little Dining Room

The Kitchen in the early 18th-century doll's house

Charles Winn, nephew of the 6th Baronet, who inherited in 1817, employed Thomas Ward to redecorate many of the rooms on the principal floor in the 1820s and contributed greatly to the collections of paintings, books and works of art. Charles's son, Rowland, created 1st Baron St Oswald, completed Adam's wing, added an attic storey of servants' bedrooms, and rebuilt the north and east ranges of the stables in 1876–7. Nostell Priory was given to the National Trust in 1954, and it is still lived in by Sir Rowland Winn's direct descendant, the present Lord St Oswald. In April 1980 a fire destroyed the Breakfast Room and damaged neighbouring rooms. In 1986 the Chippendale furniture and some other important contents were also transferred to the National Trust, through the generosity of the family and a grant of £6,100,000 from the National Heritage Memorial Fund.

In 2002, additional key chattels, the stable building, remaining part of the pleasure grounds and parkland were acquired by the National Trust, with the benefit of a £4,200,000 grant from the Heritage Lottery Fund. Service rooms, on the ground floor of the house, including the Kitchen and Butler's Pantry are gradually being opened to visitors and the parkland was made accessible for the first time in 2003.

Room unfinished.

to complete the interior in the newly fashionable Neo-classical style. Adam designed the Library, Tapestry Room, Saloon and Top Hall, and redecorated most of Paine's rooms. The figurative painting was carried out by Antonio Zucchi, the plasterwork by Joseph Rose the Younger, and the furniture by Thomas Chippendale.

Robert Adam also designed the south and west ranges of the stables, the lodges in the park, and the shell of the family wing at the north-east corner of the house in 1779–80. He planned to add three other similar wings (two of them replacing Paine's detached pavilions on the south), but the building work came to an abrupt halt after the death of the 5th Baronet in 1785, leaving the interior of the north-east wing and the Top Hall and Tapestry

Chippendale's chinoiserie pier-glass and green lacquer commode in the State Bedroom

TOUR OF THE HOUSE

The Interior

THE LOWER HALL

The Lower Hall was the usual entrance to Nostell, and was at the centre of much of the everyday activity in the house, as it was surrounded by servants' quarters and informal living rooms. In the 1830s T. F. Dibdin 'entered the lower or ground apartments and saw servants and children flitting in all directions'. To the left was the Butler's territory, with his Pantry and the Servants' Halls, and to the right, the Housekeeper's domain, together with the Muniment Room (where estate papers were stored) and other family apartments. In the 18th century 'Sir Rowland's Dressing Room and Closet' and the

'Common Eating Room' were also situated on the ground floor, as were 'Master Winn's Room' and the 'School Room'.

The main room, with its arched screen, Doric columns and pedimented fireplaces, was designed by James Paine in the late 1740s, but the outer vestibule was remodelled by Robert Adam in 1777. In the late 18th century, the Lower Hall doubled as a games room for the 6th Baronet and contained a billiard-table and cribbage board. In the 19th century, when a more formal Billiard Room was formed upstairs, it was filled with old oak furniture, and by 1902, in the 2nd Baron's time, the walls were hung with big game trophies, collected during his travels in Africa. Staff and family gathered here at Christmas and New Year for traditional

The Lower Hall, which was the everyday entrance to the house

The furniture consists largely of 17th-century oak items, including four refectory tables, two extremely fine Portuguese chairs upholstered in stamped leather, and a collection of chests and chairs in characteristic Yorkshire and Derbyshire styles. These pieces were collected by Charles Winn in the 19th century, reflecting his antiquarian

FURNITURE

entertainments from the Ackworth mummers or the hand bells of the parish ringers. For many years, oars and rowing sculls hung in the back part of the room ready for impromptu boating trips on Middle Lake, and a battery of ships' cannons (two of which remain) were kept in the Lower Hall, to be fired in the park at times of national or family festivity.

Sir Thomas More and his Family; by Rowland Lockey after Holbein, 1592 (Lower Hall)

activities. Most of the items are genuinely of an early date, but the two settles in the west passage (which you will see later on the tour) are 19th-century fabrications, made up from parts of 17th-century beds and chests.

The apothecary's counter in the south hall was supplied by Thomas Chippendale in 1771 for £19. It may have been part of the original furnishings for a 'Drug Room' in the stables.

SCULPTURE AND CERAMICS

The marble Roman statues of Silenus and a Bacchante in the alcoves at either end of the vestibule date from the 2nd century A.D. They were repaired for the 5th Baronet by the sculptor Joseph Nollekens in 1777. In the early 20th century man-sized stuffed bears stood in their place.

The incised slab represents the head of Margaret Roper, daughter of Sir Thomas More and distant relation of the Winn family, and was made by Mary Gillick in 1934. Gillick worked for the Royal Mint and designed the head of Elizabeth II used on the coinage in the 1950s. The bronze bust by David Williams-Ellis is of Derek Winn, 5th Baron St Oswald.

The pair of massive Berlin tin-glazed pottery vases was purchased by Charles Winn from Mr Pratt, a Bond Street dealer, in December 1864. The pair of large Italian tortoiseshell and ivory vases was also acquired by Charles in the 19th century.

PICTURES

The painting at the far end of the Lower Hall depicts *Sir Thomas More and his Family*. More was a lawyer, writer and leading intellectual at Henry VIII's court. He was executed in 1535 for refusing to accept the King's divorce from Catherine of Aragon and the break with Rome. This is perhaps the most famous image of early Tudor family life, showing More with his father (in red) and children and their pets. Holbein painted the original version (now lost) about 1527. In 1592 Rowland Lockey produced this large-scale copy, which has been at Nostell since the 18th century and has always been considered one of the glories of the collection. It was acquired with a grant from the HLF.

The other paintings include several portraits of 16th- and 17th-century English kings and queens, collected by Charles Winn in the same antiquarian spirit as the oak furniture.

SERVICES

The '8 large globe lamps on wrought brass scrolls & shades to ditto, supported with brass scrolls with pine apples and other ornaments nearly finished and burners complete', were supplied by Chippendale for the inner part of the Lower Hall in 1771.

The mechanical servants' bells, outside the door to the old servants' hall beyond the foot of the south stairs, date from the 1870s. To their left remain three bells belonging to an earlier system, labelled 'Hall', 'Dining Room' and 'Breakfast Room'. There is a secondary set of late 19th-century bells in the attic storey outside the servants' bedrooms.

Turn left out of the Lower Hall to the South Staircase.

THE SOUTH STAIRCASE

Paine laid out the rooms around two grand rectangular staircases in a symmetrical arrangement derived from baroque houses of the late 17th and early 18th centuries. The South Staircase was for the use of visitors, serving the State Bedroom and other guest rooms at the south end of the principal floor. The staircase itself was probably completed by June 1747, when the 4th Baronet's steward wrote: 'Before Mr Pain went away yesterday morning he drawed the form of a banester for the south stare case.' The banisters originally had lights attached, with glass globe shades similar to those in the Lower Hall.

PLASTERWORK

The plasterwork on the walls and ceiling was designed by Paine. The wall panels, providing the framework of the design, may have been executed by the plasterer and carver John Renison, who is referred to on one of Paine's drawings. However, the additional enrichment was probably carried out by Joseph Rose the Elder and his partner, Thomas Perritt. Rose and Perritt collaborated with Paine at the Doncaster Mansion House in the same period.

The decoration in the ceiling, with its tightly packed scrolls and foliage, is in the rococo style, which was very fashionable in the mid-18th century. Paine assimilated the style during his studies at the St Martin's Lane Academy in London, and his rococo work at Nostell is amongst the earliest in a house in the North of England. Chinoiserie was a feature of rococo decoration, and the heads of four mandarins, with garlands of roses hanging from their long moustachios, are concealed amongst the scrolls in the corners of the ceiling. The doorcases on the half-landing have unusual, completely detached cornices.

DECORATION

Analysis of paint samples in the 1980s indicated that Paine's original decoration was in a neutral stone colour, allowing the staircase to be seen as a continuation of the space of the Lower Hall. The present colour scheme, dating from 1988, was

The Top Hall, which Adam designed as a formal entrance hall

THE TOP HALL

Like most Palladian villas, Nostell was designed with the main entrance hall on the central axis of the first floor or _piano nobile_, approached by a grand flight of steps on the outside. This idea was never well suited to the English climate, and the Top Hall was used as a music room in the 19th century.

The early 18th-century white marble cistern at the head of the stairs was probably intended for use as a wine-cooler in the State Dining Room.

The sofas and chairs on the landing, covered with crimson cut velvet, are part of a larger set and date from the mid-18th century, in the time of the 4th Baronet.

designed to be in keeping with Paine's scheme, though the delicate plasterwork has been picked out in off-white for the best visual effect.

PICTURES

The pictures include portraits of the d'Hervart family, relations of the 5th Baronet's Swiss wife, Sabine.

FURNITURE

The gilt-bronze hanging lantern with its hexagonal body is attributed to Thomas Chippendale. Although it is not mentioned in surviving accounts at Nostell, it corresponds closely to one of his designs in the 1762 edition of _The Gentleman & Cabinet Maker's Director._

In the early 20th century, the 2nd Baron St Oswald furnished the Top Hall as a sitting room, conveniently situated between the family apartments in the north-east wing and the Breakfast Room. It became the favourite gathering place for family and friends, as the large rooms on the west side of the house were rarely used in the inter-war years. After the Second World War, the 4th Baron used the Top Hall as his office.

THE 18TH-CENTURY ADAM HALL

Paine's ground plan shows that he had intended a small alcove between the Top Hall and the Saloon, but Adam took this idea much further. Enlarging the alcove, he created a small curved vestibule between the two rooms, a very large niche on the inside of the Top Hall, and two oval lobbies either side of it leading off to the north and south. It is one of his most theatrical spatial arrangements, providing an impressive entry to the grand rooms on the first floor.

The decoration was designed by Adam in the

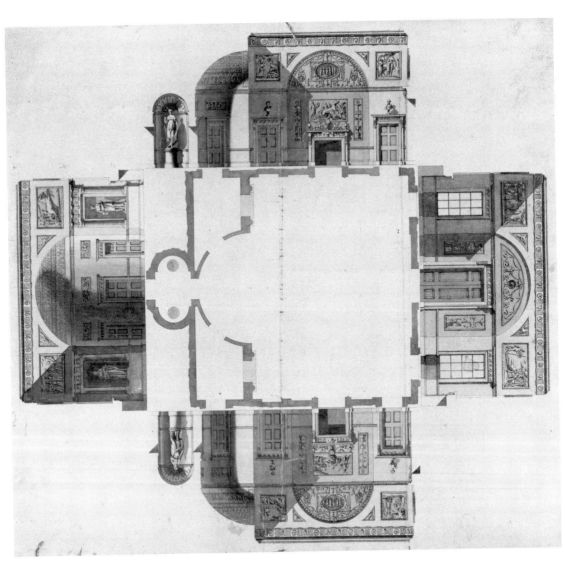

Adam's 1771 design for the walls of the Top Hall

fashionable Neo-classical style, partly based on the buildings he had studied in Italy in 1755–8. The large alcove, for example, is reminiscent of the decorative ornament on Hadrian's Villa at Tivoli, while some of the ornamental motifs show Etruscan influence. The decorative plasterwork on the walls and ceiling was executed between 1774 and 1776 by Joseph Rose the Younger, who was employed on all of Adam's interiors at Nostell. It was the largest item in Rose's account, costing £334 14s 3½d.

Key elements of Adam's elaborate plans for the Top Hall were never executed. His drawing for the walls, dated 1771, indicate that the panels over the doors, windows and chimneypieces, which today remain blank, were to be filled with

large-scale figurative subjects by Antonio Zucchi. A drawing of 1776 shows a design for a brown and white marble pavement floor, reflecting the pattern of the ceiling in the manner of Adam's other marble halls at Syon and Kedleston, but it was never laid.

Paint analysis undertaken after the fire in 1980 suggests that in Adam's time the Top Hall was decorated entirely in off-white. The paintwork was never finished, but it was clearly intended as a neutral colour scheme in tones of white, appropriate for such a grand architectural space.

THE TOP HALL IN THE 19TH AND 20TH CENTURIES

Charles Winn employed Thomas Ward, a London-based decorator and upholsterer, to redecorate the Hall between 1819 and 1821. Ward's bills record

The Top Hall in the 1870s, when it was dominated by a massive organ (now in Wragby church)

that the walls were painted in 'two tints of cream' and the ceiling in 'two tints drab colour', whilst the plasterwork was picked out in 'two tints of cinnamon coloured brown'. The floor was also renewed at this time, the present oak floorboards probably replacing coarser timber boards intended as a base for Adam's marble flags.

In the 1820s, a large organ, now in Wragby church, was erected in the Top Hall in front of the north fireplace. For the rest of the 19th century it dominated the room, which T. F. Dibdin described in the 1830s as 'a music-room of dimensions sufficiently ample for the notes of an organ, and the human voice, to reach all ears and move all hearts'. The painting of *Thomas More and his Family* was placed over the south fireplace in the 1830s and remained here until 1980.

In 1982 the National Trust repainted the Top Hall in a neutral colour scheme, approximating to Adam's intentions, whilst allowing for changes by Ward. The room was refurnished in the style of the 18th century, with the furniture originally designed for the room arranged around the walls.

CHIMNEYPIECES

The stone chimneypieces were executed in 1773 to Adam's design by Christopher Theakston of Doncaster. The cast-iron grates and the matching inner steel fender on the north fireplace are signed by Maurice Tobin of Leeds, who made several other grates and fenders in the house and also worked at Newby Hall in Yorkshire. The larger brass fenders date from the early 19th century.

FURNITURE

The eight hall-chairs, with the Winn crest painted on the backs, were supplied by Chippendale about 1775. Originally painted in a lead white colour to go with the walls, they were grained by Thomas Ward in 1819.

The pair of magnificent pier-tables supported by caryatids holding garlands of husks, which read as part of the wall decoration, was designed by Adam and probably made by his own craftsmen. An inventory of 1818 suggests that Adam never supplied the marble slabs. Like the chairs, the tables were originally painted white, but they were given green marble tops and grained by Ward in 1819.

SCULPTURE

In Adam's original designs, the oval niches and the alcoves in the vestibule are shown with life-size classical statues, which have since disappeared.

LIGHTING

The glass ceiling lights in the oval lobbies and vestibule may be the 'lamps with lines and tossels for the lobbies on each side of the Hall', referred to in a letter from Chippendale to the 5th Baronet in 1781. The present colza-oil lamp and similar lamps in the Saloon and State Dining Room were supplied in the 1820s by J. G. Litchfield of Bruton Street, London.

THE BREAKFAST ROOM

Breakfast rooms were a new feature of country-house life in the 18th century. Mrs Catharine Cappe, who stayed at Nostell in the 1760s, described the 4th Baronet's morning routine:

It was his constant custom to rise early in the morning; in winter, long before daylight, and to kindle his own fire. His letters were usually written before the family breakfast, which was always exactly at nine o'clock and he afterwards gave audience to a crowd of various descriptions of person, in succession, who were generally in waiting for his assistance and advice.

She contrasts his habits favourably with those of the young Sir Rowland, 5th Baronet, and his wife: 'Their very late, irregular hours, breakfasting at twelve or one, dining at seven or eight, were very uncomfortable, and … we sometimes made morning calls after the families we visited had already dined and were guilty of many other eccentricities.'

Like all the rooms at the southern end of the house, the Breakfast Room was designed by Paine in the 1740s and '50s. The room is described as the 'Anti or Yellow Breakfast Room' in 1818. It was redecorated by Thomas Ward for Charles Winn in 1819, when the ceiling was painted with 'enrichments to the cove' including '4 subjects from Homer painted in white relief upon circles', in the late Neo-classical style. During the 19th century,

The Breakfast Room

informal dinners were served in the Breakfast Room and it is described 'as a dining room [for] when Lord and Lady St Oswald have not many people staying' in *The World* of 1902. The Breakfast Room continued to function as a family dining room until the 1950s, when it was furnished as a sitting room by the 4th Baron St Oswald. In April 1980 a fire destroyed the room and all its contents.

RECONSTRUCTION AFTER THE FIRE

After the fire, the ceiling cove, carved doorcases and window architraves were remade following Paine's surviving drawings. The ceiling cove is a particular feature of Paine's work, found in all his rooms at Nostell. The flat of the ceiling is also based on a Paine drawing, though it has been much simplified, dispensing with his elaborate plaster-work enrichments. The carved wooden rococo-gothick chimneypiece, designed by Paine, was brought down from one of the bedrooms on the second floor.

The room was redecorated on the evidence of the 18th-century accounts. Ward's accounts record that the 'Yellow Breakfast Room' was stripped of old damask', which may well refer to the 'yellow embossed flock paper' supplied by Chippendale in 1768. In 1982, it proved impossible to imitate early methods of flocking, and so the present yellow damask-pattern paper was specially printed for the National Trust. The pattern is based on fragments of a slightly earlier red flock paper, found in the Crimson Room next door. The yellow brocade curtains and pelmet boards were made at the same time.

FURNITURE

All the present furniture was brought into the Breakfast Room after the fire.

The George III mahogany break-front bookcase may be the 'Very large mahogany bookcase with glass doors and a pediment top', supplied by Chippendale for 'Sir Rowland's Green Dressing Room' (the present Billiard Room) in 1766.

The side-chair with padded back used by the room steward is part of a set of twenty 'parlour chairs' supplied by Chippendale for Sir Rowland, 5th Bt's London house in 1766, which can be seen throughout the house. The mahogany half-sofas on either side of the fireplace, upholstered in floral cotton, also date from the 1760s.

The giltwood pier-glass with Gothic cresting,

(Left) The Persian Sibyl; studio of Guercino (Breakfast Room)

(Below) The Procession to Calvary; by Pieter Brueghel the Younger, 1602 (Breakfast Room)

THE CRIMSON ROOM

This has always been used as a guest bedroom. The architectural features of the room, including the deep ceiling cove, window architraves, cornice and doorcases, were designed by Paine for the 4th Baronet about 1750. It was originally decorated with red flock wallpaper.

Adam added the shallow plasterwork ornament to the flat part of the ceiling, and the carved rams' heads, husks and *patrae* (discs) to Paine's plain chimneypiece about 1775. In an inventory of 1806, the room is called 'the Yellow Bedroom' and it may have been redecorated by Adam *en suite* with the Breakfast Room, in Chippendale's yellow embossed flock paper'.

The Crimson Room was known by the family as the 'Amber Room' throughout the 19th and most of the 20th century, despite several changes in colour scheme. Paint analysis revealed that the woodwork and dado were painted in black in

The Crimson Room

two mahogany card-tables and cedarwood serpentine blanket chest date from the mid-18th century. The mahogany writing-table, with turned end supports and bar feet, was probably made by the firm of Gillow & Co. about 1820.

PICTURES

The large painting on the north wall opposite the chimneypiece of *The Procession to Calvary* is by Pieter Brueghel the Younger, signed and dated 1602. Like most of Brueghel's work, it was inspired by his father's sweeping landscapes, full of animated figures in contemporary Flemish dress, who almost swamp the central scene of Christ carrying the Cross. It has been at Nostell since the 18th century and is one of the finest pictures in the collection.

the mid-19th century, possibly part of a 'black and gold' colour scheme referred to in contemporary accounts. The slender plasterwork garlands of husks were applied to the dado panelling in the mid- to late 19th century and were originally gilded.

The room was also seriously damaged in the fire of 1980 and was totally redecorated over the next two years. The present crimson room wallpaper is based on the fragments of Paine's red flock paper which were discovered beneath the door frames. The wallpaper is printed in the colours of the original flock, but not enough remained to make an exact copy. The pattern was taken from a paper of very similar character and date, discovered at All Soul's College, Oxford in the 1920s and now in the Victoria and Albert Museum.

Chippendale's clothes press of 1767 in the Crimson Room. He insisted on this piece of furniture being sent to Nostell by land rather than sea to protect it from damp

FURNITURE

The mid-18th-century four-poster bed, with its rococo pierced cresting, may have been designed by Paine, whose drawings for a rather similar bed survive in the archives. After the fire, the bed-hangings and window curtains were replaced with modern crimson damask, based on an 18th-century pattern. The drapery of the bed, with its unusual 'reeded' curtains, is derived from a drawing for the hangings of a bed in the Nostell archives, probably made by a York upholsterer in the 1740s or '50s. The festoon window curtains have upholstered cornices matching the tester of the bed, which was the usual practice in the 18th century.

The large dressing-table to the left of the door to the Breakfast Room was made by Chippendale at a cost of £12 10s. It is described in his accounts on 3 July 1769 as being fitted with 'a writing drawer and slider cover'd with Green cloth with conveniences for Shaving and Cupboard with folding doors and neatly carv'd and very good locks'.

The mahogany serpentine-fronted clothes press with 'best wrought handles' was supplied by Chippendale in 1767 for £37, probably for Lady Winn's apartment. The original marbled lining paper for the sliding shelves has survived intact. Sir Rowland wanted to save money by having the new furniture sent from London by sea, but Chippendale replied that he would prefer to use the land route, since 'the damp of the ship affects the drawers and locks of good work which is made very close'.

The mahogany ribbon-back settee, which con-verts into a bed, is in the style of Chippendale. It was part of a larger set of seat furniture, acquired by the 1st Baron St Oswald in 1883, when 18th-century furniture was back in fashion. The six matching chairs were destroyed in the fire.

Other items of furniture include the George III mahogany tallboy to the left of the chimneypiece, the mid-Georgian mahogany blanket chest and the Chinese black and gold lacquer cabinet, which was probably acquired by Charles Winn in the 19th century.

THE BATHROOMS

The two small bathrooms are both decorated with hand-painted Chinese wallpaper. The early 19th-century paper in the first was probably put up when the doorway was created between the two rooms to improve access for servants.

The wallpaper in the second bathroom is of a different pattern, and more delicately painted. It matches the paper in the adjoining State Dressing Room and State Bedroom and was supplied by Chippendale in 1771. The tiny chimneypiece, carved with urns and rosettes, was inserted by Adam at the same time as the wallpaper.

The bathrooms were described as little 'Dressing Rooms' with wash-stands and dressing-tables in 1818. The present baths and basins were installed in the early 20th century.

PICTURES

At the bottom of the north wall, on the right-hand side, is *A Scene from 'The Tempest'* painted by William Hogarth about 1736. It depicts Act I, Scene 2 of Shakespeare's play: Miranda is being courted by Ferdinand (on the left) and the half-human Caliban (on the right). Her father, Prospero, stands behind, while the music-making spirit Ariel hovers overhead. It was acquired by the 5th Baronet from the sale of Lord Macclesfield's London house in 1766. More recently, in 2002, it was acquired by the National Trust from the Winn family with full funding from the National Art Collections Fund.

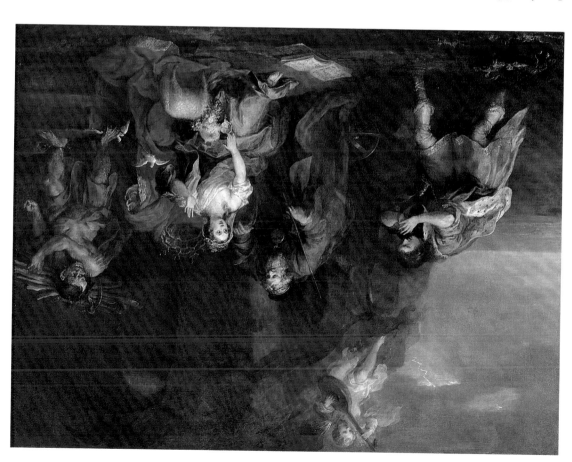

Scene from 'The Tempest', by William Hogarth, c.1736 (Crimson Room)

for the 5th Baronet between 1769 and 1771, as well as the rooms on either side to match. Adam made the bed alcove smaller and framed the niche with two Ionic pilasters. He also installed a new fireplace made of carved wood and marble.

In April 1771 Chippendale supplied 18 sheets of 'fine India paper' for three rooms of the State Apartment. (Such papers were called Indian, because they were often imported by the East India Company, but are in fact Chinese.) The wallpaper is now much faded, but it was originally painted with every sort of bird from peacocks to pheasants in brilliant blues, pinks and greens, on a white ground. By the 1770s, the exotic chinoiserie and rococo styles were considered too frivolous for a grand reception room, but suitable for a bedroom. Chippendale offered a complete decorating service, supplying the carved 'green and gold' border to

The State Dressing Room

THE STATE DRESSING ROOM

The State Dressing Room, with its bed alcove, beautifully carved Venetian window and plain coved ceiling, was designed by Paine for the 4th Baronet as the principal bedroom, reserved for the most important guests. (It was given its present name in the late 19th century, when a four-poster bed was introduced next door.) In Paine's floor plan, it is mirrored by a room at the opposite end of the house (now part of the Billiard Room), which was possibly intended as the main family bedroom. Adam and Chippendale redecorated the room

the wallpaper, the carved window cornice with lambrequin (fringed) border, and all the furniture, as well as fitting bed-hangings, curtains and carpets.

FURNITURE

The green and gilt japanned chinoiserie furniture is part of a set supplied by Chippendale for the State Apartment in 1771. It is one of the most complete and well-documented collections of furniture by the best-known English cabinetmaker of the 18th century.

The 'Dome Bedstead Japan'd Green and Gold', specially designed with 'its feet posts as Near as posable together to give as much room as posable to pass by', cost £54. It is carved with a lambre-quin border to match the window cornice. Chippendale's accounts record that the bed-hangings, window curtains and other upholstery were originally made of chintz 'lined with green persian', and tiny fragments of an 18th-century hand-painted Chinese cotton chintz have been found on the tester of the bed. Chippendale did not supply the fabric, which may have been acquired twenty years earlier by the 4th Baronet. The latter wrote to Sir Edwin Lascelles of Harewood House in December 1746 about a chintz fabric for 'the bed and furniture of one of the apartments in the new house', which was purchased through Sir Edwin's brother in Bengal. The present fabric was specially painted for the National Trust in 1982, replacing Edwardian drapery damaged by smoke in the fire. It is based on the fragments of original cotton chintz, using similar Chinese cottons in the Victoria and Albert Museum to establish a general design.

The lady's dressing-table, dressing-stool and six chairs with Chinese fret arms and Neo-classical legs, painted in green and gold, and the overmantel mirror all belong to the original set of Chippendale furniture.

The George III mahogany tallboy with Chinese trellis cornice is not part of the original set, but it is listed in the State Dressing Room in 1806.

CERAMICS

The oriental ceramics include two large early 19th-century Canton *famille rose* vases and a late 17th-century Kangxi *famille verte* deep bowl.

THE STATE BEDROOM

Paine conceived this room as a drawing room. His ceiling, with its deep cove, is decorated in the flamboyant rococo style, with putti playing musical instruments, including a lute, cello and flute.

In 1771 the room was redecorated with Chinese wallpaper and furnished as the 'State' or 'Best Dressing Room'. It became known as the State Bedroom only when the bed was introduced, probably in the late 19th century.

In the early 19th century, Charles Winn lived a relatively quiet domestic life, but his son Rowland, raised to the peerage as 1st Baron St Oswald in 1885, moved in high-ranking circles. The 1st and 2nd Barons St Oswald held grand house parties at Nostell, especially during the flat racing season, and the new State Bedroom was allocated to the most important guests. In 1902 *The World* commented that 'not many private houses in the kingdom are provided with such luxurious sleeping accommo-dation'. During a house party in 1936 this room was occupied by the Duchess of Westminster, while the State Dressing Room next door was given to the Countess of Jersey, the Crimson Room to the Marquess of Londonderry, and numerous other bedrooms on the second floor to society friends.

CHIMNEYPIECE

Paine's chimneypiece, with heavy overmantel and scrolled pediment, is of a traditional Palladian type, though the scrolling ornament and garlands of roses on the overmantel are in the progressive rococo style.

The overmantel picture of *The Canale di Cannaregio with the Palazzo Surian-Bellotto* was painted by Joseph Nicholls about 1749. This view of Venice is in the style of Canaletto, and may have been copied from a print of his work, but the hills in the background are Nicholls's own invention.

FURNITURE

The clothes press, dressing-table, dressing-stool, sofa at the foot of the bed, eight armchairs, easy chair by the fire and 'very neat Commode for the

The State Bedroom

Pier', all painted in green and gold, and the superb pier-glass above the commode 'in a very large border'd Chinese frame Richly Carv'd and finish'd', are part of the suite of furniture supplied for the State Apartment by Chippendale in 1771.

When the Chippendale collection was acquired by the National Trust in 1986, the chinoiserie suite was in particularly poor condition, and a programme of conservation was launched in 1988, funded with grant-aid from English Heritage. The commode was the most complex item, requiring 1,200 hours of skilled conservation work. The approach to the work was one of minimum intervention, using reversible materials, and great care was taken to analyse the original surface finish and find a suitable method for reproducing it.

The elaborate State Bed with its domed canopy and Edwardian floral printed cotton hangings, is much later in date, painted in green and gilt to match the Chippendale furniture.

The green lacquer chinoiserie chest of drawers from the Chippendale suite in the State Bedroom. The startlingly bright original colour is preserved on the inside of the doors

The State Dining Room is the best of Paine's surviving interiors at Nostell

THE STATE DINING ROOM

In the 18th century this room was usually used for grand entertaining. Everyday meals would have been served in the Common Eating Room on the ground floor. During the 19th century, Charles and Priscilla Winn ate in the Breakfast Room when they were alone, but they regularly entertained local friends and family here. As both the State Dining Room and the Breakfast Room were a great distance from the Kitchen in the south-west pavilion, a lift was installed in the 1870s to shorten the journey. Food was collected from a hot-plate in the Kitchen on trolleys and placed in a hot-box in the lift shaft, just outside the State Dining Room door, ready for serving.

The State Dining Room is the most complete and impressive of Paine's interiors at Nostell. The plasterwork ceiling, executed by Joseph Rose the Elder about 1748, is decorated with fashionable rococo ornament. In contrast, the walls have strong architectural features in the earlier Palladian style, particularly the chimneypiece and pedimented picture frames, giving the room an air of mas-culinity. Originally, the central window had a

CERAMICS

A selection of Kangxi and 18th-century Chinese-style dishes is displayed over the doors.

The pair of large Japanese, Arita jars and covers on the clothes press and trumpet shaped vases on the commode date from the late 17th or early 18th-century. They are one of the most important surviving groups of their kind in this country.

pedimented cornice to match the picture frames.

Paine intended the panels in the window wall to be filled with large rectangular pier-glasses, but it may have proved too expensive and difficult to obtain such a large area of glass.

Paine's decorative scheme celebrates the abundance of nature. The central panel in the ceiling is of Ceres, goddess of agriculture, with putti fishing, ploughing, hawking or making a fire in the four corners. The cornice has a frieze of vines and satyrs' masks, and the side-tables, also by Paine, are carved with goats' masks, all associated with the worship of Bacchus, the god of wine.

In 1772 Adam removed the pedimented window cornice and designed the arabesque ornament for the wall panels. The roundels over the doors were probably painted by Antonio Zucchi in the 1770s, though the frames belong to Paine's scheme. The six roundels represent allegories of leisure and are some of the most playful and decorative of Zucchi's pictures, reflecting the spirit of the surrounding rococo work. In the 1820s Thomas Ward over-painted Adam's arabesque panels and 'shadowed' the ornament, giving it a heavier appearance.

CHIMNEYPIECE

The heavy marble chimneypiece is carved with tapered pilasters mounted with classical busts and cornucopiae (horns of plenty). The carved wooden overmantel, with its scrolling broken pediment, is decorated with swags of fruit and game (with a shotgun concealed in the left-hand swag) and crowned with a basket of fruit and flowers.

The overmantel picture is a 'capriccio', or fantasy, of classical Roman ruins, including Trajan's Column, the Colosseum and the Arch of Constantine, painted by Joseph Nicholls c.1750.

DECORATION

The National Trust repainted the room in 1967, with the advice of the interior designer John Fowler. Paint scrapes were taken to help determine the mid-18th-century colours, and the present decorations are an interpretation of Paine's original scheme. Ceres and her attendants are now shown against a blue sky and the ornament on the picture frames stands out gilt against the off-white walls.

THE SALOON

THE 18TH-CENTURY SALOON

The Saloon was the principal state room on the central axis of the house and would have been approached through the Top Hall. With its high, decorated ceiling, imposing architectural ornament and large pictures inset in the walls, it was intended to provide a grand setting for large gatherings and dances, rather than for everyday life.

PICTURES

The full-length portraits of Sir Rowland Winn, 4th Bt, and his brother, Colonel Edmund Winn, painted by Henry Pickering, dominate the room. Sir Rowland, the builder of the house, stands at the far end and is shown with the new Nostell behind him. Both frames are crowned by the Winn eagle and coat of arms; Sir Rowland's is decorated with the mask of Mercury, god of trade and commerce (the source of the family's wealth), while Colonel Winn's bears that of Minerva, goddess of war.

FURNITURE

The white-painted sideboards were designed for the room by Paine, though the mahogany tops and brass rails are later additions by Adam.

The set of mahogany dining-chairs with claw-and-ball feet of the 1740s has always been in the room.

Ward introduced most of the other furnishings in 1819, including the four large pedestals for the candelabra, the carpet and the pelmet bars for the curtains.

The long extending dining-table, probably by Gillows of Lancaster, also dates from the early 19th century. The table was clearly not made for its current location, since it is longer than the room when fully extended. The fashion for large fixed dining-tables emerged only in the very late 18th century. In Paine's time the room would have been furnished with one or two smaller tables that could be folded away, and the chairs placed against the walls.

(Right) The Saloon

Adam's 1770 design for the Saloon ceiling. The colours finally adopted were green, pink and sky blue, with porphyry for the small medallions, and stone for the large medallions

Paine started work on the Saloon just before the 4th Baronet died in 1765, and the cove of the ceiling was probably part of his design. Adam substantially remodelled and redecorated the room for the 5th Baronet in the Neo-classical style between 1767 and 1776. In May 1770 Sir Rowland's agent wrote that 'Mr Rose has finished the frame round the sealing in the Saloon and a great part of the work is done in the cove'. The ceiling and walls were painted in 1773, and Zucchi finished the pictures and roundels for over the doors in August 1776, but the furniture did not arrive until after 1785.

Adam slightly lowered the height of the ceiling to fit his design and created the niche containing the door to the Top Hall, framed with Ionic pilasters. He designed most of the decorative plasterwork, but Zucchi sketched out the medallion for the centre of the ceiling, representing *Apollo's Horses watered by the Hours*. He painted the same subject for the actor David Garrick, in the front room of another Adam house, 3 Adelphi Terrace, London, a few years later.

As Adam planned it, the room would have been simply furnished, with two pier-glasses, two pier-tables and a set of sofas and chairs and 'very seldom more than a small carpet in the middle of the room'. Chippendale specified where each piece should stand around the edge of the room, and that the seat furniture was 'to be covered with green taberay [silk]', to match the colour of the walls.

THE SALOON IN THE 19TH AND 20TH CENTURIES

During the 19th century, the Saloon was used as a sitting room, a place for afternoon tea with family and friends. Ward repainted the walls and ceiling in 'tints of drab and stone' in the 1820s. A mid-19th-century photograph shows that the room was comfortably furnished, with a large leaf-pattern carpet and a great number of tables and chairs assembled in clusters in the middle of the room. The Chippendale chairs were disguised in floral-printed loose covers to give an impression of ease and informality.

The Saloon was still occasionally used for big family gatherings, such as a party to celebrate the marriage of Charles Winn's eldest son, Rowland, to Harriet Bumares in 1854. The family doctor records, 'On the return of the bridal pair from their honeymoon abroad a gay ball was given at Nostell at which Mrs Wright and I were present and where I first saw a "Tempête" danced merrily around the Saloon'. In the 20th century, the Top Hall, rather than the Saloon, was used as the principal living room.

The present decoration dates from the late 19th or early 20th century, when there was a revival of interest in Robert Adam, and the pastel shades in the ceiling were thought to be typical of his work.

PICTURES

The four paintings set into the walls are some of the largest ever painted by Zucchi. The two square panels in the east wall are 'capriccios' of classical architecture with antique figures, and the two rectangular ones over the fireplaces are of Italianate landscapes with figures dancing among classical ruins.

CHIMNEYPIECES

Adam designed the two chimneypieces, with their friezes of stylised honeysuckles and urns, in 1772. They were probably made by John Deval the Elder and installed in 1774.

FURNITURE

Many items have been introduced since the 18th century, but the original set of 18th-century furnishings remains in the room. The magnificent pier-glasses and tables were treated as part of the architectural decoration and designed entirely by Adam in 1775. The intricate scagliola and marble table tops were made by Richter and Bartoli in 1777. They cost £157 10s, more than any other item of documented furniture in the house, reflecting the status of the room. The plasterwork ornament for the pier-glass frames, with 'Sphynxs resting' and 'husks at bottom' was executed by Joseph Rose the Younger, for £12 9s 6d, with extra charged for the medallions in the crest.

The set of two settees and eight chairs was designed for the Saloon by Chippendale in 1774 in consultation with Adam. The carved curtain

Adam's 1775 designs for the pier-tables in the Saloon

The Adam ceiling in the Tapestry Room

cornices are in a similar style to those in the State Bedroom and Dressing Rooms and must have been supplied by Chippendale.

The lady's writing-table of tulip and rosewood, with a retractable fire-screen at the back, was supplied by Chippendale in June 1766 for Lady Winn's apartment and is his earliest identifiable piece in the house.

The commode to the left of the central alcove has been attributed to John Cobb. It is essentially rococo in form; the only Neo-classical feature is the inlaid vases. It was altered in the 1820s by Ward, who 'etched with black the engraved lines' and entirely renovated the inside.

The commode on the right was made by Chippendale, who charged Sir Rowland £40 for it in 1770. It is inlaid with Neo-classical urns, husks

THE TAPESTRY ROOM

THE 18TH-CENTURY DRAWING ROOM

Adam designed this room from scratch. The ceiling decorations were marked out in October 1767, and the eight fan-shaped lunettes and central panel painted by Zucchi were installed at the end of 1774. Most of the ornament in the ceiling is painted in decorative colours, and Joseph Rose's bill for the plasterwork came to a relatively modest

and *paterae* and is slightly later in style than the first.

The burr-walnut and marquetry two-manual harpsichord is by Jacob Kirckman, one of the fore-most makers of the 18th century. It was supplied to the 5th Baronet in September 1767 for £91 10s.

£87 3s 2¾d, half that of the Library. Zucchi's central panel represents *The Education of Cupid by Venus and the Muses*, and each of the lunettes show him being tutored by a muse in a different skill.

Adam's wall scheme, with twelve decorative pilasters, was largely swept away in the early 19th century, but Zucchi's rectangular pictures and two of his roundels survive, the former fixed over the doors and the latter over the pier-glasses. In April 1767 Adam wrote that 'the Drawing Room is intended to be hung with damask'. Sample silks for the walls were sent to Lady Winn, and this is the only room where there is concrete evidence that she was involved with the decoration and furnishing. It is feminine in character, intended to be rich in colour and texture, with real silk wall-hangings and splendidly painted walls and ceiling. Adam made the floorboards of 'clean deal', which was cheaper than oak, knowing that they would be completely covered with a carpet. Its rich decoration contrasts with the restrained, masculine schemes applied to the Hall, Saloon and Library in the same period.

THE 19TH-CENTURY TAPESTRY ROOM

Adam's scheme was left incomplete after the 5th Baronet died in 1785. The silk fabric for the walls and upholstery had still not been chosen in 1781, and the room is described as the 'Unfinished Drawing Room' in the 1818 inventory.

The decoration was completed in the 1820s, when Charles Winn acquired a set of Brussels tapestries to hang on the walls. The tapestries were purchased in France by an acquaintance, Warren White, in 1818, after the chaos of the French Revolution and the Napoleonic wars had dispersed many great collections, and such items were readily available. Three of the tapestries, dated 1750, are by Pierre Van Der Borcht, from a set of *The Four Continents*, but the fourth representing *Europe* was burnt in 1920 and replaced by another Brussels tapestry after a Teniers design, now on the wall adjacent to the Salon. The smaller tapestry over the chimneypiece, depicting *The Death of Achilles*, is also Flemish.

Charles Winn employed Ward to hang the tapestries between 1822 and 1824. Ward removed

The late 17th-century French cabinet in the Tapestry Room is attributed to Pierre Golle, one of the greatest designers of the period

Zucchi's pilasters and wall-paintings and stained the tapestries over 'wood framed panels'. The hangings were originally bordered with sixteen panels painted with 'festoons & 16 drops of coloured flowers', which were removed in the early 20th century. Ward also repainted the decorative parts of the ceiling in 'Permanent pink', 'Deep Naples Yellow Green' and 'Green and Crimson' and inserted four new arabesque panels into the central umbrella.

During the 19th century, it became known as the Tapestry Room, and was treated as a 'dress drawing room', used only on special occasions. The ceiling was repainted in 1977 by the Winn family, following subsidence caused by coal-mining on the estate.

fireplace has been attributed to the French crafts-man Pierre Golle, one of the leading cabinetmakers of the early part of Louis XIV's reign. It was an heirloom of the d'Hervart family and came to Nostell through the 5th Baronet's wife in 1781. A customs inventory for the goods brought over from her home at Vevey in Switzerland describes it as 'a cabinet supported by columns and six Moors at the front, representing the temple of Jerusalem, filled with drawers containing various shells and other objects'.

The smaller, Flemish tortoiseshell and ivory cabinet on the opposite wall also dates from the 17th century. It is inset with marble panels, painted with Roman capriccios, including the Forum and the Pyramid of Cestius, and was probably acquired by Charles Winn in the 19th century.

The late 18th-century commodes flanking the chimneypiece are north Italian, with marquetry in the Neo-classical style of Giuseppe Maggiolini (1738–1814).

SCULPTURE

The large marble statuary group of *Flora and Zephyr* is by Richard Wyatt (1795–1850), who worked in Rome in the Neo-classical style of his master, Canova. It was exhibited at the Royal Academy in 1834.

The paired marble pugilists on the chimneypiece are copies of Canova's celebrated sculptures in the Vatican Museum and were acquired by John Winn in Rome in 1817.

THE LIBRARY

THE 18TH-CENTURY LIBRARY

The Library was the first room at Nostell to be designed by Adam: his drawings are dated 1766. The 5th Baronet took a keen interest in the progress of the work, which was completed relatively quickly, before the end of 1767. He inspected Zucchi's paintings *in situ* before giving his approval and sent back the oval panel in the chimneypiece, finding it 'not high enough finished as it is so near the eye'. The nine paintings, set high in the upper walls, are more crudely painted and have less depth

Flora and Zephyr, by the Neo-classical sculptor Richard Wyatt, 1834 (Tapestry Room)

CHIMNEYPIECE

The white marble chimneypiece is one of Adam's most distinguished designs. It is carved with an oval medallion, depicting a scene from the story of Cupid and Psyche, containing the theme of love.

FURNITURE

The room was never furnished in the 18th century, though the mahogany and rosewood Pembroke table 'with a very good backgammon Table fitted as a drawer' had been supplied by Chippendale in 1769. It cost £7 10s, and the ivory men and dice £1 10s extra. The pier-glasses were supplied by Ward in 1824. The giltwood seat furniture was made in France in about 1820 and may also have been provided by Ward.

The large late 17th-century ebony, marble and marquetry cabinet on the wall to the left of the

The Palladian-style Library desk is one of Chippendale's masterpieces

than the oval panel at eye-level. Their theme is classical learning. Those in the upper walls show ancient philosophers and poets, while the chimney-piece panel represents *Minerva presenting the Arts of Painting, Sculpture and Architecture to Britannia*, in an interesting mixture of classicism and patriotism.

In the 18th century, the ceiling, walls and book-cases were all painted in light green, pink and white. The original scheme is accurately recorded in the portrait of Sir Rowland and Lady Winn, painted in 1767, immediately after the Library was completed, and currently displayed in the room. The room is shown without a carpet or window curtains, as Adam specifically advised Sir Rowland against the use of 'mats or carpets which contract dust and is not at all good in a book room'. The floor remained uncarpeted until the 19th century, but Chippendale supplied 'Green lustring [silk] curtains' in 1768.

THE 19TH-CENTURY LIBRARY

The present graining of the bookcases and lower walls to resemble bird's-eye maple was probably carried out by Thomas Ward in the 1820s. The books were accumulated by the Winn family throughout the 18th and 19th centuries, but they particularly reflect the antiquarian interests of Charles Winn. Charles was a keen bibliophile and bought numerous books on antiquities, architecture, early local history, medieval studies, numismatics and natural history. The archive includes hundreds of bills from booksellers, including William Pickering of Piccadilly, London, who was described in 1848 as 'a sort of Golconda [an Indian city famous for its diamonds] to him who looks for diamonds of antiquity'.

Winn also amassed a collection of antiquities, curiosities and natural history samples, many of which were kept in the Library. The cupboards under the bookcases were filled with items as varied as ancient pottery, fragments of fossilised bone, a skull and a Roman sandal, many of which can now be seen in the Museum Room. From the late 19th century, visitors were invited into the room to view these accumulated curiosities, and one noted in 1902 that it was 'reminiscent of Napoleon the First, for it contains the double-barrelled flint-lock presented to him by the gun-makers of Paris [and] a

FURNITURE

The furniture has changed little since Adam's time and includes all the items originally designed for the room by Chippendale between 1766 and 1768. In the centre of the room is a massive library-table, the single most expensive item made by Chippendale for Nostell, at a cost of £72 10s. It is clearly shown in Hamilton's painting and is considered one of Chippendale's masterpieces. Given its date, its decoration is surprisingly old-fashioned and instead of Neo-classical or even rococo motifs, it is ornamented with lions' heads and paws in the earlier, Palladian style.

Chippendale also supplied the six library chairs with lyre backs, costing £36 for the set, the 'metamorphic' stool, which turns into library steps (£14), and the artist's table fitted with cupboards

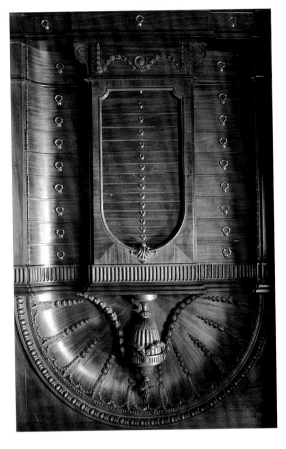

The medal cabinet in the Library

likeness of him on ivory done in his own hair that was on his bed in St Helena'. The hair portrait of Napoleon can still be seen on the mantelpiece. The 2nd Baron also kept a parrot in the Library 'with a very choice vocabulary', which was apt to startle his guests.

PRESENT DECORATION

The upper walls and ceiling were redecorated in 2000, replacing an unsympathetic scheme of 1977. The redecoration is based on a late 19th-century scheme, derived from detailed paint analysis and documentary research. It was chosen because it both complements the graining of the bookcases and closely accords with Adam's original intention for the ceiling.

CHIMNEYPIECE

The marble chimneypiece was supplied by John Deval & Co. in July 1767. The wooden relief panel of putti inserted above, representing the various Arts, was carved by William Collins.

PICTURES

The portrait of the 5th Baronet and his wife by Hugh Douglas Hamilton was commissioned in 1767 for their house in St James's Square and came to Nostell in 1785, when the London property was sold. Hamilton has doubled the size of the Library, to provide a suitable background for the figures, by painting the south wall in line with the west wall and omitting the fireplace.

SCULPTURE

The six busts over the bookcases were introduced in the late 19th century. Two of the busts, representing the head of the Venus de' Medici, date from the 18th century. They are very similar to the bust on the pedestal in the painting and may have been provided by Hamilton in the 1760s as ornaments for the house. The rest were supplied by Brucciani & Co. in the 19th century.

SILVER

The large silver inkstand, on the Chippendale desk, engraved with the Winn crest, was made for the 5th Baronet by Mark Cripps in 1769.

and drawers (£85). The second artist's table has been attributed to Chippendale, though it does not appear on his account.

In addition, Chippendale designed a medal cabinet for the Library, which is concealed behind the door to the right of the chimneypiece. Both the 5th Baronet and Charles Winn collected ancient coins and seals, which were stored in the cabinet's numerous drawers.

The pier-glasses were designed by Adam and the plasterwork frames made by Rose.

The Billiard Room, which also houses the overflow from the Library

In the event, the north-west wing was never built, and the north-east wing was left unfinished until the late 19th century, so the room never became a vestibule. It was eventually turned into a billiard room by Charles Winn in 1819. A few years later, the paintings were replaced with bookcases, to accommodate Charles's collection of books, which had quickly outgrown the Library. At the same time, the Venetian window was reglazed and fitted with French doors, probably intended to open on to a balcony, which was never executed. A second tier of bookcases was installed in the room in the 1870s.

In 1972 the National Trust repainted the room, with the advice of the late John Fowler, using a combination of terracotta and biscuit colours.

THE BILLIARD ROOM

This became the Billiard Room in 1819, and before then had been through several changes. Paine conceived the room as a grand bedroom only half its present size, but he later made plans to turn it into a library. When the 5th Baronet inherited, he established a new Library in its present location and commissioned Adam and Chippendale to decorate this room as his own 'Green Dressing Room'. He appears to have shared a bedroom with his wife in the room next door. Between 1767 and 1771 Adam designed the plasterwork ceiling in the inner section of the room, and Chippendale's accounts record that the 'Dressing Room' was 'hung with plane green paper and gilt rope border' and 'My Lady's [Sabine Winn's] picture fixed over the chimney'. It was furnished with 'a very large mahogany bookcase with glass doors and a pedi-ment top', together with a matching clothes press. Sir Rowland's Green Dressing Room was barely finished when Adam formulated proposals for enlarging the house in 1776. The 5th Baronet's dressing room moved to the ground floor, and this room was extended outwards by 21 feet into a 'T' shape, to serve as a vestibule to the proposed new wings at the north end, Adam designed the plaster-work in the extension in 1783, and its simple Grecian ornament is noticeably later in style than the elaborate decoration in the Top Hall and Saloon, dating from the 1770s. In the late 18th and early 19th centuries, the first section of the room was densely hung with pictures, including Sir *Thomas More and his Family*, and the room is called 'The Picture Gallery' in the 1818 inventory.

CHIMNEYPIECES

Adam designed the chimneypiece in the inner part of the room between 1767 and 1771 and that in the extension in 1783. The inset plaster panel above the fireplace in the extension, depicting Paolo and

THE DRAWING ROOM

Francesca, the doomed lovers from Dante's *Divine Comedy*, was made by Richard Westmacott the Younger in 1837.

FURNITURE

The billiard-table is a rare 18th-century example, its cushions stuffed with sand and is probably that listed in the Lower Hall in 1806.

The longcase clock which stands between the two sections of the room was made in 1717 by John Harrison, the son of the estate carpenter at Nostell. The mechanism is almost entirely made of wood, with the movement, frame and wheels in oak, the pendulum in mahogany, and the spindles and pinions in boxwood. Harrison later became famous for inventing the first timekeeper accurate enough to determine longitude at sea and after a long struggle received a reward of £20,000 from the government for his creation.

The set of ten armchairs, covered in red leather, is the 'mahogany french arm chairs stuff'd and cover'd with blue Morine' made by Chippendale in 1767 for Lady Winn's Blue Dressing Room (now the Little Dining Room). The mahogany library-table, with adjustable easel, also dates from the late 18th century.

The bookcases and the settee under the window of the 1820s have been attributed to the firm of Gillow & Co. The bookcases were bought from a sale at Stapleton Hall in Yorkshire and installed here in 1833. They were accepted in lieu of Inheritance Tax by H.M. Government and allocated to the National Trust in 2002. The two specimen marble tables, one with a circular and the other with an octagonal top, were probably bought by John Winn in Rome while on the Grand Tour.

THE DRAWING ROOM

Paine originally designed this as a family bedroom, and the architectural ornament and heavy statuary marble chimneypiece belong to his scheme. It may have been the 4th Baronet's own bedroom, as an 'Inventory of Beds' of 1763 records that Sir Rowland, a widower, slept alone on the 'Principal Storey', while his daughters had bedrooms on the second floor, and his son at ground level. After the 5th Baronet inherited, the room was redecorated as a bedroom for himself and Lady Winn, with Sir Rowland's Green Dressing Room and Lady Winn's Blue Dressing Room on either side.

Chippendale handled all the furnishing and decoration of the room, charging for hanging the room with Chinese wallpaper in December 1769. He supplied 'a large bedstead with mahogany feet posts and carved cornices with cotton furniture', 2 window curtains to match the bed' and window cornices carved with a lambrequin (fringed) border, which remain in the room.

The room was redecorated by Charles Winn just prior to his marriage in 1819 and was used as a bedroom until 1986, when it was redecorated as a drawing room by Denise, Lady St Oswald. The red colour of the walls was chosen to show off the pictures in their fine carved and giltwood frames.

FURNITURE

The oval giltwood pier-glass, with its magnificent cresting of bell-flower swags and scrolling foliage, is one of a pair made by Chippendale for Lady Winn's Bedroom and Dressing Room, invoiced on 2 November 1767 for £50. The other one is in the Little Dining Room next door.

The 'mahogany Lady secretary made of very fine wood, a bookcase top' was supplied by Chippendale in June 1766, probably for one of Lady Winn's rooms. The secretaire cabinet itself cost £25, and the detachable side cupboards, which arrived several months later, cost £5 5s. The serpentine commode with ormolu mounts was supplied by Chippendale in April 1770, costing £7 17s 6d.

The set of six armchairs and two sofas, the frames carved with bell flowers, date from the 1780s or '90s. They have been attributed to Thomas Chippendale the Younger, though there is no record of their purchase at Nostell.

PICTURES

The large painting in the middle of the south wall of *Angelica hesitating between the Arts of Music and Painting* is a self-portrait painted by Angelica Kauffman in Rome in 1791. As a girl, she had been advised to pursue an operatic career, but she decided on painting, for which she had shown

THE LITTLE DINING ROOM

In the 18th century, Lady Winn probably used this room as a boudoir in which to entertain select groups of friends. During the 19th century it became a family sitting room. It was furnished as a private dining room by the 4th Baron in 1953 and is still used when the family is in residence.

DECORATION

Once again, the shell of the room was designed by Paine, but was redecorated by Adam as 'Lady Winn's Blue Dressing Room' in the 1760s. The painted decoration on the ceiling and doors dates from Adam's time and has elements of the Pompeian style, derived from the Roman frescoes unearthed at Pompeii and Herculaneum in the mid-18th century. The figurative panels in the ceiling were executed by Zucchi, including the oval in the centre of Cupid and Venus and the medallions in the four corners of putti at play. The decoration

Angelica hesitating between the Arts of Music and Painting, by Angelica Kauffman, 1791 (Drawing Room). As a young woman, she could not decide whether to become an opera singer or a painter

exceptional talent at an early age. The figure of Painting (in blue) points upwards to the Temple of Fame – which she achieved, becoming one of the only two female founder-members of the Royal Academy. It was acquired by the 2nd Baron St Oswald from the Cokethorpe Collection in 1908 for 650 guineas and originally displayed in the Top Hall. Kauffman was associated with Nostell through her marriage with Antonio Zucchi in 1781, and in the 19th century several of Zucchi's paintings were attributed to her hand. The large still-life painting of food, a jug and glasses on a table, on the west wall, is an exceptionally fine example by the Dutch artist, Pieter Claesz, dated 1640. Both this and the Kauffman painting were acquired in 2002 by the Pieter Claesz Trust, with a grant from the Heritage Lottery Fund.

The Little Dining Room

Chippendale's accounts record that the room was 'hung with blue verditure paper and a small goodcroon [gadrooned, ie fluted] border, gilt in burnish gold' and 'two very large drapery window curtains of blue moreen [a wool fabric]'. Verditure, a plain bluish-green hand-coloured wallpaper, provided an ideal background for pictures, and in the 18th century the walls were densely covered with oil paintings, as they are today. Chippendale supplied 41 picture frames 'gilt in burnished gold' for the room, some of which remain on the walls.

Charles Winn commissioned Thomas Ward to redecorate the Blue Dressing Room between 1819 and 1821. Ward painted over the wallpaper in a grey-blue colour and installed the present fireplace, inset with different coloured marbles. Otherwise, he left most of the 18th-century decoration intact, only retouching the white ground colour to the

on the cove was painted on paper, cut out and then applied.

ceiling and repainting the arabesque ornaments of 6 doors and 6 door caps', in a style faithful to Adam.

PICTURES

The six pictures over the doors by Zucchi represent the story of the lovers Angelica and Medoro. Zucchi selected the subject-matter himself, writing in a letter to Sir Rowland in 1772 that he would 'endeavour to chuse objects that may be agreeable to her Ladyship's taste'. In Ariosto's poem *Orlando Furioso*, Angelica is loved by Orlando (or Roland), a Christian knight who is fiercely jealous of Medoro, and the legend may have been chosen as a compliment to Sir Rowland Winn.

The painting of *Cleopatra and the Asp*, after Guido Reni (1575–1642), above the chimneypiece depicts the Egyptian queen committing suicide with the bite of this poisonous snake. It was purchased for the room by the 5th Baronet for £18 15s at the sale of Lord Macclesfield's London house in 1766. Sir Rowland considered it one of the gems of his collection, and it was given pride of place over the

fireplace. The frame, 'richly carved and gilt in burnished gold, with exceeding rich carved and gilt ornaments', was specially designed by Chippendale and cost £34 10s., more than any other in the house. It was altered by Thomas Ward in the 1820s, when the elaborate cresting, matching that of the pier-glass, was removed to store. The remains of the crest were rediscovered in the 1980s and can now be seen in the Museum Room.

FURNITURE

The dining-table and the set of four urns and pedestals originally stood in the State Dining Room, but were removed during the 1820s alter-ations and came here in the 1950s. The three sections of the mahogany dining-table allow it to be used in different ways. It is transitional between the smaller, more flexible tables of the earlier 18th century and the long telescopic dining-tables of the 19th century, illustrating changes in eating habits. The urns and pedestals were made by Séfferin Nelson in 1772, probably after a design by Adam. The oval pier-glass, with elaborate giltwood frame, is the pair to that in the Drawing Room next door, and was supplied by Chippendale in 1767. The pier-table under the pier-glass has an early 18th-century base, heavily carved with scrolls and swags, but the mahogany top was added at a later date. The set of eleven dining-chairs and two carvers, with splat backs carved with ears of wheat, may have been supplied by William Skurray, an uphol-sterer of Wakefield, in 1794, for a ground-floor eating room. The mahogany bow-fronted sideboard, inlaid with chequered lines, dates from the early 19th century.

THE NORTH STAIRCASE

The North Staircase was originally designed as the family staircase, leading to Sir Rowland and Lady Winn's apartment at the north end of the principal storey and the bedrooms on the second floor. Paine completed it just before the South Staircase in 1747. The rococo plasterwork ornament is similar to that of the South Staircase, but, surprisingly, is more elaborate, considering the other was intended for guests.

The decoration of the top landing and ceiling contains several references to the Winn family. The spread eagle, crest of the Winns, perches at the top of the wall panel, holding a garland of flowers in its claws, and hovers dramatically in the centre of the ceiling. The eight roundels over the doors contain portrait medallions of members of the family, the frames decorated with flowers for the women and husks for the men. The heads of Henry VIII and Elizabeth I, hidden amongst lavish ornament in the ceiling, probably commemorate the former's anti-monastic policies, which enabled the Winns

The Adam-style decoration on the Little Dining Room doors was repainted by Thomas Ward in 1819–21

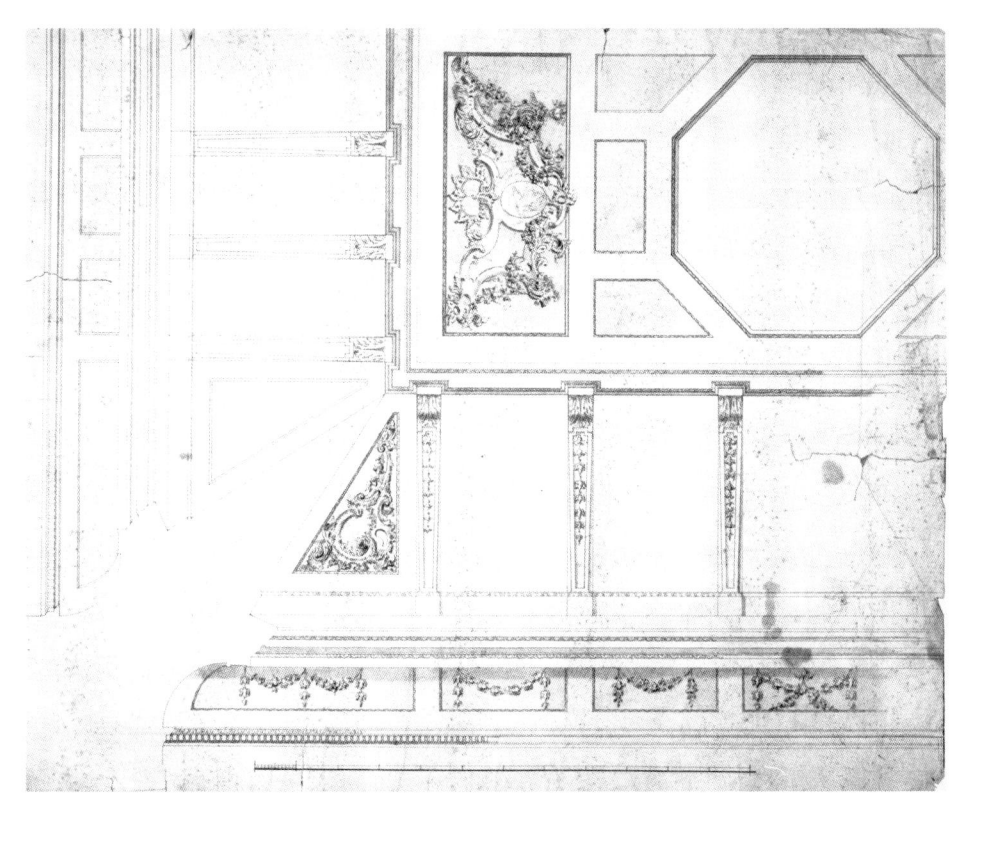

Paine's c.1747 design for the ceiling of the North Staircase

to acquire Nostell Priory, and the foundation of the family fortune by George Wynne, Draper to Queen Elizabeth.

The hunting trophies on the wall of the second flight of stairs, with masks of a fox and hound, may also have a special significance. Mrs Cappe records in her memoirs that 'a pack of fox hounds was kept [at Nostell] not so much for the amusement of their master [4th Baronet], although he was himself partial to the exercise of hunting, as for a sort of rallying point, that should draw around it the neighbouring gentlemen'.

FURNITURE

The barometer by Justin Vulliamy, at the head of the first staircase, is one of the most important pieces of furniture in the house. Its 'very neat case … made of fine tulip, and other woods and very rich carv'd ornaments Gilt in Burnish Gold and plate glass in the doors' was made by Chippendale in 1768–9 at a cost of £25.

The mahogany break-front library bookcase on the first landing is one of four supplied by Chippendale for Sir Rowland's London house about 1766. The pair of chinoiserie giltwood metal wall-lanterns on either side of the bookcase dates from the second half of the 18th century. The side-chairs are the remainder of the set already seen on the South Staircase.

The hanging lantern is modern and was designed to complement the Chippendale one on the South Staircase. It was funded by the Friends of Nostell.

Turn left at the foot of the North Staircase and walk towards the servants' staircase. With the servants' staircase on your left, turn right into the Muniments Room.

THE MUSEUM ROOM

This room was designed as an office by Paine in the 1740s, but it was turned into 'The New Eating Room for the Steward and Company' by Adam in the 1770s. It was used as a dining room for the upper servants, which in the late 18th century included Mr Dawson, the Steward or Land Agent, Mr Smallpiece, the Butler, Mr Peruzze, Sir Rowland 6th Baronet's valet, Mrs Wilment, the Housekeeper and Mr Jacques Armand, Lady Winn's Swiss cook. The Steward's Dining Room was allowed three large candles for lighting every other night in winter, and it was the Porter's duty 'to wait at the Steward's Room table, to clean the knives, lay the cloth &c'.

Today the room is used as a Museum Room, displaying the famous Nostell Doll's House, a collection of antiquities, an armorial service and a selection of architectural drawings.

DOLL'S HOUSE

The doll's house was made for the Winns about 1735, around the time of the building of the 4th Baronet's new house, and the pediment bears a cartouche with his arms and those of his wife, Susanna Henshaw. The accuracy of the architectural ornament on the exterior and the attention paid to every aspect of the decoration and furnishing of the interior, suggest that the doll's-house was made by professional craftsmen as a model for adults, rather than as a child's toy. According to family tradition, it is the work of the young Thomas Chippendale, who was born at Otley, only a few miles away from Nostell, but there is no real evidence to support this.

The interior is decorated in the style of the mid-18th century, with almost all its original furnishings. The ground floor contains an Entrance Hall, Parlour and Kitchen; the first floor, a grand apartment, with Red Velvet Bedroom, Chinese Dressing Room and Drawing Room, decorated with contemporary French prints; and the attic storey, family bedrooms. All the fireplaces in the house are copied from James Gibbs's *Book of Architecture* (1728) and each item of furniture is made with incredible precision. The 'white lacquer' cabinet in

THE MUNIMENTS ROOM

The Muniments Room was created out of James Paine's Stone Parlour' or 'Common Eating Room' in the years from 1776, when the 5th Baronet wrote a memorandum to Robert Adam concerning, "A room for keeping the family writings". Muniment rooms were the equivalent of a modern archive system used for storing 'muniments' or documents with a legal significance.

The Nostell Estates and family papers kept in this room would have been used by the family and by senior servants such as the steward. Although many of the rooms on the lower floor were purely service rooms, the 5th Baronet clearly saw this as his own business room and had his own adjacent dressing room and closet. Usually this type of room, serving a functional purpose, tended to have a basic form, but the Muniments Room at Nostell Priory is remarkable for its elaborate surviving fittings. Its status is illustrated by two finely decorated 18th-century keys, labelled for the muniment bookcases, which are very similar to the key for Adam's bookcases in the Library.

The handsome architectural bookcases were made for the room and were originally painted in an elaborate colour scheme with off-white grounds and mouldings picked out in pink against a deep green field. Although structurally altered for Charles Winn, when the cases were deepened and painted cream, the cabinet interiors retained traces of the Adam colour scheme. Some of the interior pigeon-holes are labelled in French, referring to the papers of the 5th Baronet's Swiss wife, Sabine d'Hervart.

Long used as a store, the room was conserved in 2004–5 and the cases acquired by the National Trust with generous funding from the Heritage Lottery Fund.

Turn right out of the Muniments Room and continue to the South Hall. To your right is the Museum Room and to your left the Servants' Hall.

*The Entrance
Hall in the
doll's house*

CABINET OF CURIOSITIES

The assemblage of antiquities, curiosities and natural history specimens was originally part of a larger collection, gathered by Charles Winn in the 19th century. The objects are extremely diverse, including ancient pottery, coins and axe heads, exotic animal bones, fossils, mineral samples and a human skull, from places as far afield as ancient Rome, Africa and the Lake District. Several have their original labels, such as the 'Roman Sandal from an Irish Bog', 'Cone from a Cedar of Lebanon', 'Bit of Rhinocerus' and 'Middle joint of the toe of the mammoth, Hyena's Cave, 23 July 1822'. Some of the items are genuine antiquities and others are 19th-century fakes. Many were bought by Charles from curiosity shops, dealers and country-house sales, while others were found on his estates in Lincolnshire and Yorkshire, or collected by friends on their travels.

ARCHITECTURAL DRAWINGS

These are facsimiles of the original 18th-century designs, which still survive in the Nostell archive, including several by Robert Adam.

CERAMICS

The china in the glass cabinets is part of a large Chinese *famille rose* armorial service, dating from about 1800. It is probably the 'Dinner and Dessert Service of China, 271 pieces' purchased by Charles Winn for £81 6s from the sale at Castle Bar Park in Ealing, in the mid-19th century. The arms, crest and motto *Per ardua alta* belong to the Hannay family.

the Drawing Room is fitted with an ivory interior, and the console table in the Parlour is made with wrought-iron brackets and a marble top. The grandfather clock in the Hall is signed 'Jno Hallifax of Barnsley'.

To the left of the chimneypiece are fragments of the cresting of Thomas Chippendale's frame for *Cleopatra and the Asp*, hanging in the Little Dining Room.

THE SERVANTS' HALL

This room is referred to as the Servants' Hall in Paine's plan of the 1730s. The Servants' Hall moved to the Brew-house Pavilion in the late 18th century, but it returned to its present location when the pavilion was demolished in the 1820s. The room was used as a dining room by the lower servants, including, in the 4th Baronet's time, Sir Rowland's Footman, Miss Winn's Footman, the Under-butler, Upper- and Under-housemaid, the Upper- and Under-laundry Maid, Store Room Maid, Dairy Maid, Taylor, Maltster and Butcher. The Gamekeeper, Groom, four Under-grooms, Coachman, Under-coachman, Postilion, Painter, Blacksmith, four 'Husbandmen' [gardeners] and Menageryman [poultry man] also ate here.

The 4th and 5th Baronet's building work increased the size of the household, and Mrs Cappe records that 'the family consisted of not fewer than sixty or seventy persons, among whom were many workmen and artificiers, who were constantly employed in it and regularly dined in the servants' hall'. With workmen constantly coming and going, the 4th Baronet instructed his porter:

Not to permit any Strangers to be Loytering in the Servants' Hall, but to enquire whom they want and then to send for that person and to be able to give me or any of the upper Servants an Account of who they are and what they want and if they cannot give some account of themselves to turn them out and to Complain to Me or to Allen or the Buttler, who shall first be met with.

CONTENTS

Part of Nostell's *batterie de cuisine* is displayed in the painted dresser with pediment top.

Exiting through the south door, turn right down the passage to the Kitchen Pavilion.

The Exterior

THE ENTRANCE FRONT

The main block presents to the park a cliff-like mass of stonework, thirteen bays wide and crowned by a tall pediment. This is the house that James Paine built from 1735, probably to a design by Colonel James Moyser, who in turn was inspired by the villas of Andrea Palladio. It is, however, a ponderous composition, with none of the lightness of its Italian models, chiefly on account of its engaged portico of Ionic columns, which gives the front a flat, two-dimensional effect, and its heavy, high-pitched roof, undisguised by any balustrade or attic. As originally designed, the central rectangular block was to have been surrounded by four satellite pavilions containing servants' quarters and other apartments, with which it was linked by curved, arcaded corridors. These would have softened the austerity of the main house, embracing welcoming forecourts at the front and back. However, only two of these pavilions were ever built, and now only one, the old Kitchen on the west front, survives. The pavilion containing the Brew-house originally stood to the south-east of the main block, almost where the iron gate is now, but was demolished by Charles Winn in 1824.

The great central pediment encloses the carved Winn coat of arms, profusely mantled in rococo ornament. This corresponds to an engraving in the archives signed by Paine and dated 1743. The imposing perron of steps that lead up to the first floor was added by Robert Adam about 1777. They originally had an ironwork balustrade, but this was replaced in stone by the 2nd Baron St Oswald about 1910. He also added the pediment over the doorway to the Lower Hall. The pinkish area of stonework around the windows to the left of the portico is a scar of the fire which devastated this part of the house in April 1980.

To the side of the main house, almost a separate Palladian villa in its own right, stands Adam's Family Wing, the only one of four pavilion-like wings which Adam proposed to add to the house

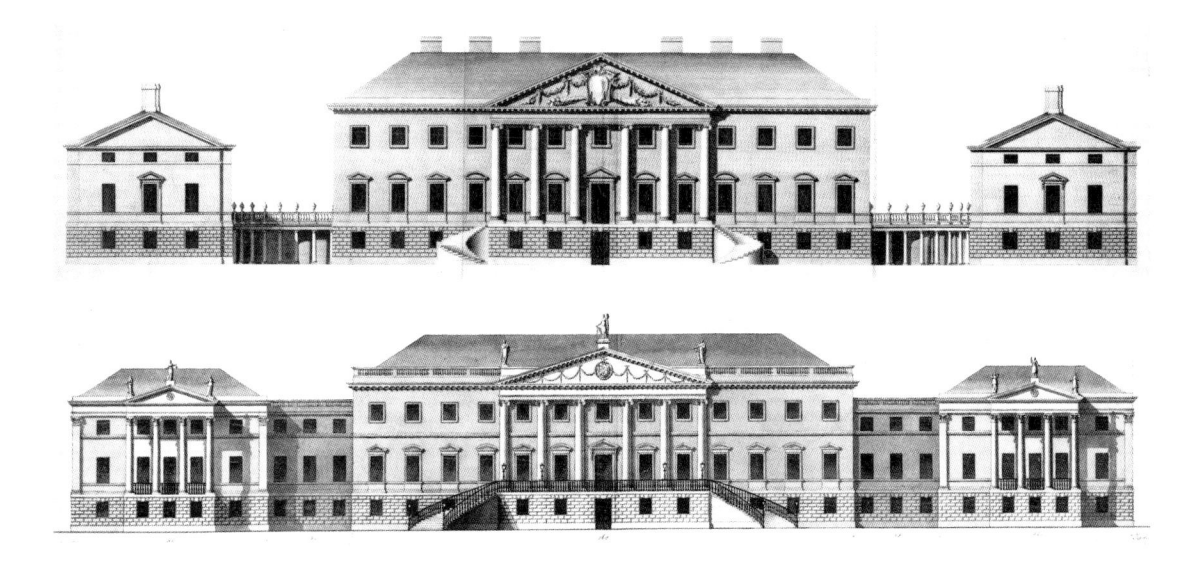

The entrance front

Designs for the entrance front by James Paine (above) and Robert Adam (below)

that was actually executed. It is a handsome structure, its projecting columned portico raised up on a high rusticated basement, providing a welcome vertical emphasis to the long entrance façade. The unusual collared Ionic order employed for the portico is derived from a prototype found on Hadrian's Villa at Tivoli, near Rome. The Family Wing was intended to provide additional accommodation for the family of the 5th Baronet. In March 1776 Sir Rowland wrote to Adam, 'We are in great want of a sett of apartments for our young family, Miss Winn having got a new Governess & we are at a loss (we have so large a house) how to fix them'. Work began in 1779 and it was roofed in the spring of 1780. However, the death of the 5th Baronet in 1785 halted the fitting up of the wing, which remained a shell until the refurbishments of 1875. Since then, it has served almost as a separate house, providing comfortable accommodation when the state rooms are not in use – a purpose it continues to fulfil from time to time even today.

THE WEST FRONT

If you approach from Wakefield, the west or garden front is your first glimpse of Nostell Priory, its façade visible through the trees from the bridge over the lake. The west front is very like the entrance front, although on this side Paine's frontispiece is adorned with flat pilasters instead of attached columns. The window surrounds are also more elaborate, those on the upper level being embellished with baroque scrolls. Paine intended the centre of the huge pediment to be carved with the Winn coat of arms, but this has never been done, leaving instead a strange, abstract composition of projecting blocks of stone.

Attached to the main block by a curved wall is the sole survivor of the two satellite pavilions which lay to the south of the house. This one housed the Kitchen until the mid-20th century and is a somewhat ungainly structure with a tall pyramidal roof. It was probably designed by Colonel Moyser. The curved passage which connects the pavilion to the main house was originally an open arcade, and was only filled in at a later date. Kitchens were frequently detached from houses in the 18th century and earlier because of the great danger of fire.

Adam made no alterations to the west front, but from 1779, as with the entrance front, he drew up ambitious plans to build flanking bow-fronted wings on either side of the central block. That on the south side was to replace the Kitchen pavilion, while the northern wing was to contain a large Music Room with a semicircular bay. These additions never came to pass, but the masonry which projects from the back of the Family Wing – the beginnings of an elaborate architectural light well he devised for the dark courtyard that would have been created between the two pavilions – shows that his plans were given serious consideration.

THE STABLES

The stables have a complex history, going through at least four stages of design, before they were finally completed in the late 19th century.

The first stables were built by the 3rd Baronet just before he died in 1722 at right-angles to, and north-east of, the old house. When the 4th Baronet decided to abandon the old Priory, he made plans for much larger stables, aligned to the main axis of the new house, but incorporating the building of 1722. The east and north ranges were constructed soon after 1763, in the last years of the 4th Baronet's life, with the earlier stable attached at a rather awkward angle on the west side of the north range. Work on the stables continued under Adam, who designed the south and west ranges for the 5th Baronet after 1766. Building work started in May 1770, when the clerk of works, Benjamin Ware, reported that he was obliged to set the Masons to prepare work for the new Stable'. The south range, which now overlooks the rose garden, ingeniously combined facilities for riding, with amenities for the pleasure grounds. The central block, with its curved loggia of three great arches, contained a Riding House, with a Greenhouse and Garden Room on either side, opening on to the lawn. The end pavilions, with pyramid roofs and Venetian windows, were a 'Drug Room' and 'Gardener's Room'. The exterior of the south range remains

The Stables

almost exactly as designed by Adam, though the interior has been substantially altered, and the Garden Room was converted into a coach-house in the 1820s.

The 5th and 6th Baronets were both keen horsemen and kept several successful racehorses in the stables at Nostell, but Charles Winn was less actively interested in the sport. Between 1827 and 1829, he employed the York architects James Pritchett and Charles Watson, who held virtually a monopoly of architectural work in the county at that time, to reduce the size of the stables. The eastern range and part of the north range, dating from the 1760s, were demolished, and a new gateway was created in the west range, crowned with a cupola built to Adam's designs of 1776. Charles considered converting the Riding House into a private theatre, but this scheme was never realised.

Fifty years later, Charles's eldest son Rowland decided to rebuild the stables to their former size. Between 1875 and 1877, he employed the architect James MacVicar Anderson to demolish the mis-aligned stable of 1722 and rebuild the east and north ranges in line with Adam's buildings. At the same time, the cupola was physically moved from the west range to crown the gateway in the north range, as Adam had originally intended. The work was completed in 1904, under the 2nd Baron St Oswald, and the stables remain much as he left them.

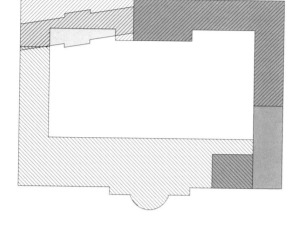

(Right) The development of the Stables

1722 3rd Baronet (demolished)

1760s 4th Baronet

c.1770 Adam

1875–7 & 1904 MacVicar Anderson

N ↑

THE PARK, PLEASURE GROUNDS AND GARDENS

THE PARKLAND

The land surrounding the house was first enclosed as a deer-park by the Gargraves in 1604. It encompassed farms and woodlands, previously owned by the Priory of St Oswald, and included a medieval pond which formed the basis of the Middle Lake today. The earlier house, converted from ranges of the original monastic buildings, was provided with a series of enclosed gardens, which were swept away during landscaping work in the 18th century. Between 1730 and 1820, the parkland was completely redesigned to provide a setting for the impressive new house built by Sir Rowland Winn,

4th Bt, and his son. The parkland today is the remnants of the 18th-century park, with later developments.

The 4th Baronet commissioned plans for formal designs for the grounds from Stephen Switzer, the leading landscape gardener of the day, and Joseph Perfect, a local nurseryman, soon after his return from the Grand Tour in 1729. Neither Perfect's nor Switzer's plans were fully implemented, but certain elements in their designs relate to the present layout of the park, most strikingly the avenue of trees that forms a long vista in front of the house. It was originally planted with elm trees in the 1730s, but they became depleted in the early 20th century and were replaced with the present sycamores.

In the late 1750s the 4th Baronet started to develop the parkland in a naturalistic style, which replaced the formal design of the early 18th century. In about 1759 he created the Upper Lake and planted trees and flowering shrubs to the south of the house. Between 1759 and 1761 he also reconstructed the public bridge on the Doncaster–Wakefield road to a design by Sir George Savile, a neighbouring squire and amateur architect. It crosses between Middle and Upper Lakes at the south-west border of the park, and can be viewed from the state rooms on the west side of the house. A commemorative poem written at the time gives 'Mr Watson and Mr Gott' as the builders: John Watson (d.1771) of Wakefield, Surveyor of Bridges to the West Riding from 1743 and father of the York architect Charles Watson; and John Gott

(1720–93) of Calverley, near Leeds, resident engineer of the Aire & Calder Navigation. The poem goes on to give the reasons for its renewal:

Thy ancient Structure now in Ruins lies,
Behold a *Phoenix* from its Ashes rise:
A noble Pile, where Ease and Grandeur's shewn,
A true *Portrait of Him* that doth thee own.

The 5th Baronet redefined the boundaries of the parkland and the means of approach to the house. He diverted the Doncaster–Wakefield road and built a high perimeter wall with superb lodges, designed by Adam as an extension of his work on the house. The most important entrance was at Featherstone, on the route from Pontefract to York, and was marked with a gateway in the form of a pyramid. The secondary entrance at Foulby, off the Doncaster–Wakefield road, ornamented with winged sphinxes, has now been demolished. The third gateway, Wragby Lodge, visible from the church and much plainer in design, was considered a back entrance until the arrival of the railway in the nearby village of Nostell in the mid-19th century. The present visitor entrance, to the east of Wragby Lodge, was created in the mid-1980s.

The bridge for the Doncaster–Wakefield road was built by the 4th Baronet in 1759–61

THE PLEASURE GROUNDS AND GARDENS

The pleasure grounds on either side of the Middle Lake to the west of the house can be explored by visitors today. A path at the north end of the house leads around Middle Lake, across the dam at the bottom end of the lake, and on to the Menagerie Garden at the far west side. The garden was established on the site of a medieval stone quarry in the late 1750s, in conjunction with the construction of the road bridge. The location of the garden may have been inspired by Switzer's plan, which incorporated a 'hermitage and cascade out of the old quarry'. The Menagerie Garden is centred on a small gothick building known as the 'Menagerie House', originally occupied by the menagerie keeper and his wife and later used as a gardener's cottage. The central portion of the Menagerie House, called the Gothick Room, with decorative plasterwork interior executed by Joseph Rose the

The Menagerie House in the 1870s

In 1808 James Hank & Co., nurserymen of Keighley, undertook a major planting scheme, completing the layout of the park. They turned the parkland into a contemporary landscape, with clumps of trees and perimeter woodland in the style of 'Capability' Brown. Lower Lake and the canal cascade from Middle to Lower Lake, suggested in Switzer's plan, were completed in the 1820s.

During the 19th century, new areas of woodland were established to provide extra cover for game birds, obscuring some of the earlier pattern of planting. The park has always been used by the Winn family for country sports. The 4th Baronet kept a pack of fox hounds on the estate, and a herd of deer grazed on the land for almost four centuries, until 1975. In 2002 the parkland was acquired by the Trust with a HLF grant, and opened to the public for the first time in 2003. It is undergoing a long-term programme of restoration and replanting.

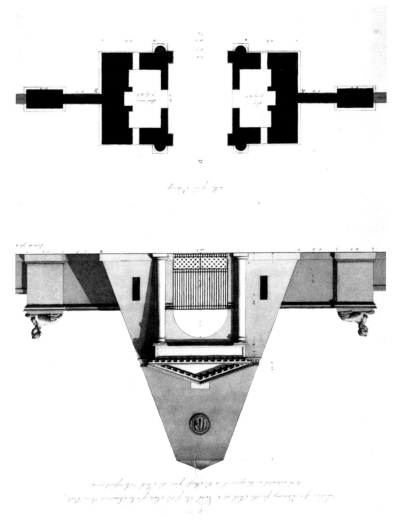

Featherstone Lodge was designed by Adam in 1776

Elder, was completed in 1765. It was probably designed by Paine, but the two side wings were added by Adam about 1776. A plan of 1758 shows that the Menagerie Garden was originally set out with a series of enclosures, which were probably aviaries. Surviving late 18th-century accounts record poultry, including turkeys, geese, ducks and drakes, which were cared for by the keepers for 12s a week. A pit for fighting cocks was constructed in the area in 1783, to the design of Francis Labron. In the mid-19th century, the garden was laid out with formal flower-beds, decorated with urns and statues, a few of which remain. More recently,

the front of the Menagerie House was replanted with climbers, including wisteria and hydrangea, in the Victorian style.

The character of the pleasure grounds today reflects the 19th century, when the area surrounding Middle and Lower Lakes was planted with rhododendrons, holly and other shrubs and conifers. Rhododendrons became a celebrated feature of the park, and local people gathered on the road bridge in early summer to admire their brilliant colours. The grounds were occasionally opened to tenants on the estate, and on the day of the annual Sunday School Feast, children and teachers were

The Rose Garden and Orangery

entertained on the lawn with a brass band and plentiful quantities of tea.

The lakes were used by the family for boating and fishing, and in 1794 the 6th Baronet constructed a boathouse at the bottom end of Lower Lake. In the 1870s a 'Swiss Bridge' was built across the cascade in the middle of the dam, on the way to the Menagerie Garden and a stone footbridge, known as the 'Druid's Bridge', at the foot of the cascade, forming part of the network of paths in the pleasure grounds. The Druid's Bridge has since collapsed and the Swiss Bridge was replaced with the present wooden bridge, not dissimilar in appearance, in the 1980s.

A separate garden area can be found to the south of the stable block. This was established in the 1770s, when Adam built the south range of the stables, incorporating a 'Garden Room' and 'Banquetting House', and was set out with flower-beds and decorative shrubs. A tennis court was added in the 19th century, and the present rose garden in the 1920s. The rose garden is bounded on the west by a wall of the Kitchen Gardens (not open), located in this area since the mid-18th century, in accordance with Switzer's and Perfect's plans. The Kitchen Gardens were greatly extended and modernised in the late 19th century, with new ranges of greenhouses to grow exotic fruits and plants, admired by contemporary horticulturalists.

Wragby church, adjacent to Wragby Lodge, was built in 1533 in the time of the old priory and is open to visitors in the park. The interior was restored and refurbished by Charles Winn and the 1st Lord St Oswald in the 19th century (see p. 60). It contains early Swiss stained glass, a 17th-century Venetian pulpit with fine wood carving, a series of family monuments, and the organ previously sited in the Top Hall.

NOSTELL PRIORY AND THE WINNS

THE MEDIEVAL PRIORY

The name 'Nostell Priory' commemorates an Augustinian priory, which had been founded in the early 12th century on a site very close to the present house. It was dedicated to St Oswald, an Anglo-Saxon King of Northumbria, honoured for spreading Christianity among his people. The religious community was abolished at the time of the Dissolution of the Monasteries in the 1530s, but the Priory buildings survived at Nostell until the 18th century.

The legend of the foundation of the medieval priory is described in the 'Nostell Act Book', a manuscript compiled in the late 14th century and translated from the Latin for the 4th Baronet in the 18th century. It records that Ralph Adlave, Chaplain to Henry I, fell ill on his way to Scotland and was detained for a while at Pontefract. During his convalescence, he came across a community of hermits at Nostell and was so impressed by their piety that he determined to establish a priory on the site and quickly obtained royal support for his project. The story contains a kernel of truth, as the Priory was created out of a pre-existing hermitage, dedicated to St James, with King Henry's encouragement, and the character 'Adlave' may be derived from 'Athelward', the first Prior, who was formerly Chaplain to the King. However, the site is more likely to have been chosen by Archbishop Thurstan of York, who actively promoted the foundation of Augustinian houses in the north of England, in an attempt to reinvigorate religious life in the area. The replacement of hermits by Augustinian canons was part of a wider strategy by the church to regularise the priesthood. The Priory of St Oswald was the most important of the northern houses, granted substantial lands by Henry I, as well as twelve pence per day from the exchequer at York and the right to hold an annual fair on the feast day of St Oswald.

The ruins of the old priory, sketched about 1777 (Bodleian Library, Oxford; Gough Maps 35 f. 31)

19th century.

The foundations of the Priory were laid by Athelward about 1122, and work progressed over two centuries. A single building survives from the medieval period, in Home Farm courtyard adjacent to Wragby Lodge. It was possibly part of the monastic Lay Brothers' yard, converted into a cow-shed and slaughterhouse in the 19th century. The other early survival is the choir of Wragby church, built in 1533 by Prior Alvered Comyn.

The Priory of St Oswald was at the height of its power in the late 13th century, under Prior William de Birstal. The Nostell Act Book records that there were 26 canons and 77 servants in the house, including 11 in the malt-house and bakery, 7 in the kitchen, 3 in the brew-house, 9 in the smithy and carpenter's shop, 5 carriers and 16 ploughmen. The Priory profited from well-stocked farms and started to work the coal seams at Nostell, which proved a great source of wealth for the Winn family in the 19th century.

THE 17TH-CENTURY HOUSE

The last prior, Robert Ferrar, surrendered the Priory to Henry VIII in 1540. The buildings and land, including 'a coal mine ... usually kept in the hands, working and occupation of the former prior of the former monastery', were granted to Dr Thomas Leigh, one of the King's appointed Visitors, for the sum of £1,146 13s 4d. From Dr Leigh, Nostell passed to Sir Thomas Gargrave, Speaker in Queen Elizabeth's first Parliament. Gargrave was one of the Queen's most trusted advisers in the North, despite trying to persuade her to marry. He settled at Nostell in 1567, and was buried at Wragby in 1579. The estate was sold to William Ireland in 1613 and in 1629 to Sir John Wolstenholme, one of Charles I's tax collectors, for £10,000. As a Royalist, Wolstenholme was one of Parliament's scapegoats after the Civil War: when a £20,000 fine was levied on him in 1654, he was immediately declared bankrupt, and Nostell was sold to the Winn family, with whom it has remained ever since.

The Winns originally came from Gwydir in North Wales, but they made their fortune as textile

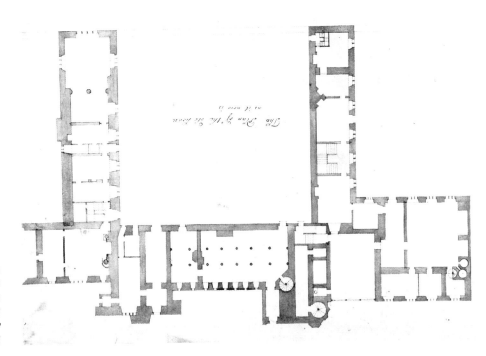

Plan of 17th-century Nostall Hall, which incorporated three ranges of the old priory

The Plan of the Old House as it now is

merchants in London. George Wynne (c.1560–1610) was appointed Draper to Queen Elizabeth I, and his grandsons, George and Rowland Winn were made Aldermen of London and Masters of the Mercers Company in the mid-17th century. As the Winn family increased in wealth, they invested their money in land. They acquired the estate and manor of Thornton Curtis in Lincolnshire in 1627 and expanded their holdings during the Common-wealth, buying the lands of defeated Royalists, including the manor of Appleby in Lincolnshire, as well as Nostell. They managed to benefit from the restoration of the monarchy, as well as the Commonwealth, since George and Rowland Winn contributed 2,000 guilders towards the Royalist cause and George was granted a baronetcy by Charles II in 1660.

Before the Winns purchased Nostell, Dr Leigh and his successors had converted three ranges of the Priory buildings into a manor house, known as 'Nostall Hall'. The house was situated slightly to the south-west of the present house, overlapping the Kitchen Pavilion, where medieval stonework can still be found in the basement. An early ground plan shows that it was arranged around three sides of a courtyard, with a large central hall, possibly created out of the monks' refectory.

Three generations of the Winns used Nostell Hall as their principal residence, continuing to live there until the early 18th century. Sir Rowland, 3rd Bt, built a new stable block before his death in 1722, but it was his son, Sir Rowland, 4th Bt, who decided to abandon the old hall and build a modern house. A large part of Nostall Hall remained standing until the late 1770s, and it was probably used by the family whilst the new house was being built. Catharine Cappe recalled great celebrations held at Christmas by the 4th Baronet in the 1760s, when 'open house was kept for 3 days [and] all the farmers and cottagers upon the estate were invited, along with their wives, to dine in the Great Hall', possibly referring to the earlier house.

THE 4TH BARONET, COL. MOYSER AND JAMES PAINE

Sir Rowland, 4th Bt, inherited Nostell in 1722, at the early age of sixteen. During his minority, the Yorkshire and Lincolnshire estates were left in the care of his uncles, while he travelled to Geneva to complete his education. In the 18th century, many young Englishmen were sent to Protestant Geneva to learn French, away from the influence of French Catholicism. From there, Sir Rowland embarked on a two-year Grand Tour of Europe, accompanied by his tutor, a French Protestant pastor, Jacques Serces. He toured Germany, Austria, France and Italy, then considered the cultural centre of Europe, where he visited the great cities of Naples, Milan, Venice and Rome. He returned to Nostell in 1727 fired with plans for rebuilding the house and laying out the park in the contemporary style. Having married Susanna Henshaw, co-heiress of a Lord Mayor of London, in 1729, and with the considerable wealth inherited from his father, he commissioned plans for an ambitious new house from the Beverley gentle-man-architect, Colonel James Moyser.

Colonel Moyser is named as the architect of Nostell in a marginal note in a copy of the Builder's Dictionary (1734) and is known to have worked elsewhere in Yorkshire, designing Bretton Park for his close friend Sir William Wentworth about 1730. He belonged to the circle of Lord Burlington, an enthusiast for the work of Andrea Palladio, the 16th-century Italian architect who inspired a gener-ation of English architects in the early 18th century. Burlington himself designed the York Assembly Rooms in the early 1730s and was probably known to Sir Rowland Winn, who was appointed High Sheriff of Yorkshire in 1731. The plan of Nostell, with its central rectangular block connected by curving corridors to four pavilions, is loosely based on Palladio's proposed designs for the Villa Mocenigo at Dolo. The Mocenigo plan had previously been adapted by Lord Burlington for Tottenham House in Wiltshire in 1721, and by William Kent, one of Burlington's protégés, for Holkham Hall in Norfolk about 1730. None of Moyser's drawings for the house

Sir Rowland Winn, 4th Bt, the builder of Nostell Priory, which appears in the background; by Henry Pickering, 1746 (State Dining Room)

survives, and, like many gentlemen-architects of his day, he probably had neither the technical knowledge nor the inclination to see his designs carried out. A drawing of a house very similar to Nostell survives by Colen Campbell, another of Burlington's favoured architects. The main block of the Campbell design, with its rather heavy and curiously unPalladian proportions, and the internal arrangement of the staircases are almost identical to the finished building. Campbell died in 1729, but it is possible that he was employed as a professional architect to draw up and execute Moyser's design, a role eventually fulfilled by James Paine.

Paine was engaged by the 4th Baronet to conduct the building work at Nostell in 1736 at the age of nineteen. In the early years, Moyser continued to advise on the project, but Paine made considerable alterations to the building on site and was given full responsibility for the decoration of the interior. He continued to work for the 4th Baronet on and off for almost 30 years and eventually published plans of the house in Woolfe and Gandon's supplement to *Vitruvius Britannicus* in 1767. Compared to the later 18th century, very few accounts of the building work under Paine survive, but Dr Pococke, visiting in 1750, found the main block of the house completed, as well as 'the grand offices of one side', referring to the two pavilions on the south, one of which has since been demolished. The two pavilions at the north end of the house were never built. Paine's letters to Sir Rowland suggest that work on the interior started in 1747 and continued throughout the 1750s and '60s. According to an 'Inventory of Beds', all the family and staff had moved into the new house by the time the 4th Baronet died in 1765, but only half the state rooms on the first floor had been finished.

Nostell was one of Paine's first commissions after completing his studies at the St Martin's Lane Academy in London and holds a place of great importance in his career. He lived in the neighbouring village of Wragby for at least eight years, while working at Nostell, and was married to a local girl in Wragby church in 1741. He subsequently established an extensive practice among other Yorkshire patrons, which brought him work in the West Riding at Cusworth, Stockeld, Stapleton,

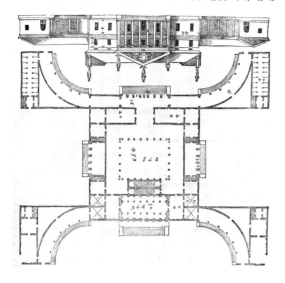

Palladio's Villa Mocenigo, which inspired Nostell

Sandbeck, Cowick and Bramham. Paine again adapted the plan of the Villa Mocenigo for Kedleston Hall in Derbyshire in 1757, and developed many of his favourite decorative motifs whilst working at Nostell. He was one of the first English architects to design interior plasterwork, previously left to Italian craftsmen, and his ceiling decorations for the Staircases, State Bedroom and Dining Room are pioneering work in the light and elegant rococo style recently imported to Britain from the Continent. The decorative plasterwork in these rooms was almost certainly executed by Joseph Rose the Elder and Thomas Perritt, who regularly collaborated with Paine.

Many of the other craftsmen who worked for Paine at Nostell remain anonymous, but surviving accounts refer to another plasterer, John Renison, Thomas Wagg, a London blacksmith, Maurice Tobin of Leeds, who supplied grates and fenders to both Adam and Paine, and Robert Barker, a York cabinetmaker, who made designs for a bookcase in 1764. Relatively few items of furniture remain in the house from the 4th Baronet's time, but they include the Dining Room chairs and the velvet-covered seats on the staircases. Paine himself designed the side-tables in the Dining Room, and his exceedingly rare drawings for other furniture, including a bed and chairs, remain in the archives.

THE 5TH BARONET AND ROBERT ADAM

The 5th Baronet and his wife, who commissioned Adam to remodel and decorate the house; by Hugh Douglas Hamilton, 1767 (Library)

Sir Rowland Winn, 5th Bt, was born in 1739. Like his father, he completed his education in Switzerland, living in Lausanne with his tutor Isaac Dulon between 1756 and 1762. Lausanne had a sizeable English population, very much as Robert Wharton described Geneva in 1775, 'brimful of English, who live truly à l'Angloise, have race horses and all their appendages', and Lord Huntingdon recalled the busy social life of the city, with its assemblies, balls and parties. Rowland caused his father considerable anxiety, spending

substantial sums of money on renting and buying horses, an interest he later manifested in building a riding school at Nostell. He must also have visited the house of the anglophile philosopher Voltaire, a place of pilgrimage for many young English gentlemen in the 1760s and '70s; he purchased *The Complete Works of Voltaire* for 30 ducats in 1757. During his time abroad, he met, and in 1761 married, Sabine d'Hervart, daughter of Baron Jacques Philippe d'Hervart, Governor of Vevey. The 4th Baronet travelled to Switzerland specially to negotiate his son's marriage.

Rowland inherited the family estates in 1765 at the age of 26, and his succession marks a crucial turning point in the history of Nostell. Rather than asking Paine to continue and complete the house, he turned instead to his new and energetic rival, Robert Adam. According to Thomas Hardwick,

*Adam's 1767 design
for the Drawing Room
chimneypiece*

'Paine and Sir R. Taylor nearly divided the practice of the profession between them till Mr Robert Adam entered the lists and distinguished himself by the superiority of his taste in the nicer and more delicate parts of decoration'. Adam was the most successful architect of the later 18th century, superseding Paine at Kedleston and Alnwick, as well as Nostell. He was extremely good at cultivating contacts and counted among his friends several members of the aristocracy. His relationship with the 5th Baronet was far warmer and more intimate than Paine's strictly professional dealings had ever been with his father. In 1772 he wrote, 'I will not pretend to describe what I feel in regard to Sir Rowland Winn & Lady Winns friendship, it surpasses all I can say', and four years later, 'We had a glorious lunch of your excellent venison yesterday when we remembered with much pleasure the founders of the feast'.

Robert and his younger brother James each spent about three years studying architecture in Rome between 1754 and 1763 and on their return to England became the unrivalled exponents of a newly fashionable style, known as Neo-classicism. The 'New Classicism' was based on an academically correct interpretation of classical art and architecture, partly inspired by recent archaeological discoveries at Pompeii, Herculaneum and elsewhere in Italy. More restrained than the rococo and less conventional than the Palladian style, it incorporated a more accurate use of the classical orders, a far wider range of decorative motifs and sophisticated spatial arrangements, all of which are evident in Adam's work at Nostell.

Adam started work on the interior of the house in 1766. Over the next decade, he created the sequence of rooms which occupies roughly the northern half of the main block, starting with the Library and progressing to the Tapestry Room, Saloon and Top Hall. He also redecorated many of Paine's interiors. The documentation of this work is almost complete, and from all the drawings, letters and bills which survive, a detailed picture of Adam's methods and his team of craftsmen can be built up. As in so many of his other commissions, the three main participants were the decorative painter Antonio Zucchi, the plasterer Joseph Rose the Younger and the cabinetmaker Thomas Chippendale.

Zucchi was a Venetian artist who had met the Adam brothers in Italy and, according to Goethe, accompanied Robert Adam and Charles-Louis

Clérisseau on their famous journey to Spalato (now Split) in 1754, contributing drawings to Adam's book on the classical ruins there. He was invited to come to England by Robert Adam in 1766, and his paintings for the Library at Nostell, completed in the following year, must be amongst the first he executed in this country, predating his work at Harewood, Kenwood, Home House in London, Newby, Osterley and Saltram. The subject-matter of Zucchi's paintings is entirely classical, with imaginary views of Roman ruins, scenes from the story of Cupid and Psyche, and other mythological stories, but his treatment of these subjects still has all the charm and grace of the rococo. His style is akin to that of Angelica Kauffman, whom he was later to marry, and his work at Nostell has often been attributed to her. This mistaken belief may have prompted the 2nd Baron to purchase Angelica Kauffman's famous self-portrait in 1908, which now hangs in the Drawing Room.

From Zucchi's correspondence with Sir Rowland Winn and his surviving drawings, it is clear that he also provided designs for the sections of plasterwork which incorporated figures, while Adam himself designed the rest of the ornament. The plasterwork was executed by Joseph Rose the Younger, nephew of the Joseph Rose who had worked with Paine. Rose the Younger was used by Adam in nearly all of his major commissions and proved himself more than an ordinary craftsman by travelling to Rome in 1768 to master the art of

classical ornament. Apart from the architectural plasterwork, Rose made the pier-glass frames in the Saloon and Library and undertook more prosaic work, repairing ceilings and laying lime ash floors in the servants' bedrooms. His full accounts at Nostell, date from 1766 to 1777, totalling £1,822 3s.

Nostell Priory is famous today above all for the contribution of the third member of this trio, Thomas Chippendale, one of the greatest English cabinetmakers. He was responsible for the complete furnishing of the house for Sir Rowland Winn between 1766 and 1785, and over 100 pieces by or attributed to him remain at Nostell. Chippendale published the first comprehensive book of furniture designs, *The Gentleman & Cabinet Maker's Director*, in 1754 and his work was widely imitated, so that it is usually difficult to establish its authenticity. At Nostell, however, a large number of his bills and letters have fortunately survived, which precisely identify many items and make the house an extremely important source for the study of his work.

The son of a carpenter, Chippendale was born in Otley in 1718, and though little is known of his circumstances until his marriage in London in 1748, his Yorkshire connections may have contributed to the success of his business. Apart from Nostell, he was employed in the county at Harewood, Goldsborough, Newby, Denton and Burton Constable, and Sir Rowland Winn and Sir Edwin Lascelles of Harewood gave Chippendale his greatest commissions. However, Chippendale's letters reveal that his relationship with his patron was far less friendly than that of Adam. Sir Rowland was often late in paying his bills, and in a letter of September 1767 complaining of goods not being delivered, threatened that 'Your Behaviour to me is not to be Bore [sic] and [I] shall take care to Acquaint those Gentlemen that I have Recom-mended you to and desire that they will oblige me in employing some other person'. Chippendale, despite his talent, was evidently treated as an ordinary tradesman, while Adam was respected as a professional man.

The Chippendale furniture at Nostell is particu-larly interesting for its diversity both in quality and style. It ranges from the expensive, magnificently carved pieces, such as the medal cabinet in the Library, to a chopping-block for the kitchen, and

Chippendale's green lacquer commode in the State Bedroom

from the conservative 'Kentian' form of the Library table, to a set of green japanned chinoiserie furni-ture for the State Apartment and to Neo-classical pier-glasses, Library chairs and a barometer frame. Some of the Chippendale furniture, such as the bookcase on the North Landing, was commissioned for the Winns' London house. In 1766 the 5th Baronet had purchased a fashionable London address, 11 St James's Square, which was refronted by Adam, and where he again used Chippendale to supply the furnishings. Apart from furniture, Chippendale also supplied and fitted wallpaper and bed-hangings at Nostell and in London, providing his client with a complete furnishing and decor-ation service.

The 5th Baronet's marriage to Sabine d'Hervart also greatly enriched the collection. When Baroness d'Hervart died in 1780, Sabine became sole heiress to the Swiss estates, and pictures, silver, linen, books and some furniture were transported from there to Nostell. Some of these items remain in the house, including the 'Temple of Jerusalem' cabinet in the Tapestry Room and several family portraits, now hanging on the South Staircase. The 5th Baronet also bought many of the paintings in the house. He was clearly an inverterate spender, on one occasion purchasing 'a coloured gold toothpick case' for £35 (half the price of the great library desk).

Robert Adam's role was not confined to the interior of the house. He also redesigned the southern and western ranges of the stables, including a large riding school and greenhouse, designed the three lodges and extended the Menagerie House. However, in 1776, before the interior of Paine's existing house was completely finished, he was given a much more ambitious project, to extend and adapt the already substantial house. Adam proposed pulling down Paine's pavilions to the south and constructing four large wings, two flanking the entrance front with large Ionic porticoes, and two flanking the west front of the house with semicircular central bays overlooking the lake. In the event, only one of the wings was ever carried out, the family wing at the north-east corner in 1779–80, and Paine's pavilions were reprieved. Adam's only alteration to the main block of the house was his remodelling of the perron in the centre of the entrance front, with two flights of steps curving down either side, designed in 1777.

Adam's work at Nostell came to an abrupt halt in 1785, when the 5th Baronet was killed in a carriage accident on the road to London. His building project was left incomplete, the decoration of the Top Hall and Tapestry Room remained unfinished, and the north-east wing was an empty shell until the late 19th century. Over half a century of building work had seriously depleted the family's financial resources. Sums of money were still owing to Adam, Chippendale and Zucchi, and the London house in St James's Square was sold in the same year, probably out of financial necessity. Henry Skrine, touring the North of England in the late 18th century, described Nostell as 'an overgrown, and yet unfinished modern house'.

THE 6TH BARONET

After the 5th Baronet died, Sabine Winn continued to live at Nostell with her two children, Esther and Sir Rowland, the 6th Baronet, a child of ten. T. G. Wright records in his memoirs that Sabine 'became very stout and was wheeled about in a quaint big wheeled chair, which was preserved in old Nostell days, as well as her poles for exercise'. Until the young Sir Rowland came of age, the Yorkshire and Lincolnshire estates were largely managed by Shepley Watson, a local solicitor, who was closely associated with the family until his death in 1830. The 6th Baronet, created High Sheriff of Yorkshire in 1799, is described by Wright as 'a gay fox hunter taking pleasure chiefly in his hounds and horses'. He was a keen sportsman and owned a number of racehorses, which he kept in the stables at Nostell. He died unmarried in 1805.

JOHN AND CHARLES WINN

The 6th Baronet's sister, Esther, married John Williamson, a Manchester baker, in 1792. The match was considered unsuitable and she was estranged from the family for many years, but the 6th Baronet provided for her three children, John, Charles and Louisa, after her death in 1803. When Sir Rowland himself died, the family estates passed to the eleven-year-old John Williamson junior, once again under the supervision of Shepley Watson. The Williamson children changed their name to Winn, but John did not succeed to the Baronetcy, which was inherited through the male line and passed out of the immediate family to a first cousin. John Winn died in Rome in 1817 whilst on the Grand Tour and was succeeded by his brother, Charles.

Charles Winn married his cousin, Priscilla Strickland, in 1819 and immediately employed Thomas Ward, a London decorator and upholsterer, based in Frith Street, Soho, to redecorate Nostell. Over the next six years, Ward repainted and furnished many of the major rooms, supplying carpets, curtains, picture frames and additional furniture and renting a house in Wakefield for part of that time. Charles also bought a substantial amount of furniture from the Lancaster firm of Gillow & Co., including probably the bookcases in the Billiard Room and the Dining Room table, though the items are not individually documented. Both John and Charles made plans to complete the building work at Nostell. Ambitious schemes for balancing the north and south ends of the house with elaborate service courtyards were drawn up by the York firm of architects Watson, Pritchett & Watson, but they were never executed, possibly for lack of money. However, in 1824, the Brew-house Pavilion at the south-east corner of the house was demolished, and the brewery relocated in a corner of the stable courtyard. Further alterations were made to the stable buildings in 1829. In later years, Charles, who had accumulated debts through

(Right) The monument to John Winn (d. 1817) by Francis Chantrey in Wragby church was commissioned by his brother and sister, Charles and Louisa Winn

adding to his Lincolnshire estates, bemoaned the burden of 'so overgrown a house' and even considered selling the property and relocating to Thornton Hall, one of his houses in Lincolnshire. In the event, the family persuaded him to remain at Nostell, and the estate at Thornton was sold in 1846.

Charles Winn had a scholarly mind and anti-quarian interests. Without the distractions of a large building project or political ambitions, he became passionately interested in collecting. He visited sale rooms, dealers and house sales across the country and travelled to London several times a year, partly for this purpose, staying in Thompson's Hotel or the University Club. Charles brought his brother John's collection of Etruscan vases back from Rome. He also bought paintings, books, antique furniture and other works of art for the house

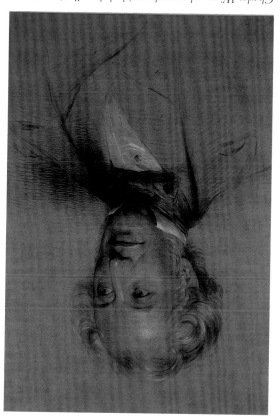

Charles Winn, who greatly enriched the collections at Nostell in the 19th century

The Saloon c.1870

and accumulated an extraordinary collection of antiquities and curiosities. In 1849 alone, he acquired 16 paintings, ranging in price from a 'Rembrandt' for 350 guineas to a portrait of *'Charles I when young'* for £2, having earlier admitted to Abraham Grace, a Wakefield dealer, 'I have more pictures at Nostell than I can hang up'. Nostell was particularly admired for its picture collection in the 19th and early 20th centuries, though a number of the paintings purchased by Charles as original Old Masters later turned out to be copies. Most of the paintings in the house today were acquired in his time.

Between 1825 and 1835, Charles Winn repaired and refurbished Wragby church, and commissioned Ward to redecorate the interior in an antiquarian spirit. He furnished the church with a 17th-century Venetian pulpit and a Norman font, taken from a ruined church in Lincolnshire. Charles also amassed an extremely fine collection of Swiss stained glass of the 16th and 17th centuries, said to have been acquired whilst travelling on the Continent, though some was bought from an Edinburgh dealer in 1828. The glass was intended for the windows of the church, and was eventually installed by his son Rowland in the late 19th century. New glass for the east window was painted by Ward's son, Thomas, who later became well known as a maker of stained glass, to commemorate the founders of the Priory of St Oswald. T. F. Dibdin, an eccentric antiquarian author, visiting in the 1830s specifically to view the church, credited Charles with 'a cultivated eye for

Chippendale furniture, which had come back into Maurice Brockwell on the pictures and the Nostell collection and commissioned a book from Pontefract. He realised the importance of the as an officer in the Coldstream Guards and MP for the family estates in 1893, having previously served Rowland Winn, 2nd Baron St Oswald, inherited saint of the medieval priory.

Baron St Oswald, choosing for his title the patron Prime Minister in 1885, Rowland was created 1st Conservatism. When Lord Salisbury was elected

An 'Ape' cartoon of the 1st Baron St Oswald, who modernised the servants' quarters and the stable block in the 1870s

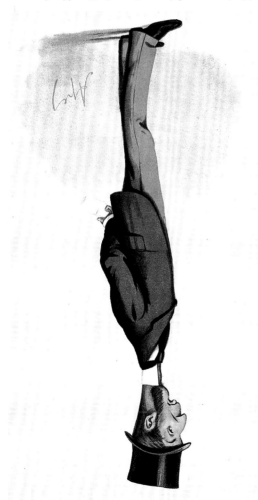

the antique'. Charles was evidently interested in the history of the Priory and it is likely that the present name of the house, Nostell Priory, was adopted in his time.

Charles Winn died in 1874 and was succeeded by his son, Rowland.

THE 1ST AND 2ND BARONS ST OSWALD

By the time Rowland inherited Nostell, the Winns' finances were beginning to improve. During the 19th century, the family started to exploit the reserves of coal on their estate, mined on a smaller scale since the medieval period. They took over the running of all their collieries and sunk new pits to increase production. In 1859 Rowland discovered ironstone on the family's Lincolnshire estate, which was combined with Nostell coal to produce steel. By 1870, the Lincolnshire works produced an income of over £11,000 per year, and the Winns had established themselves as successful industrialists.

Between 1875 and 1877, Rowland embarked on a major programme of rebuilding and refurbishment at Nostell, under the direction of James MacVicar Anderson of Stratton Street, London, nephew of the Scottish architect William Burn. The north and east ranges of the stable block, partly dating from the 1720s, were rebuilt, and T. G. Wright records that the house 'which sorely needed repair, was renovated, re-painted and enlarged and it resumed its former splendour'. The north-east wing was finally decorated and furnished, and the attics were converted into additional staff accommodation. The Kitchen Pavilion, larders, laundry, dairy and other domestic offices were refurbished and the services updated, with a hydraulic lift and improved system of bells. The house was converted to electricity about 1890.

Rowland Winn was MP for Lincolnshire for seventeen years and pursued a successful political career, serving as Conservative Chief Whip and Lord of the Treasury in the 1870s and '80s. He held party rallies in the grounds at Nostell, and the house became known as a centre for northern

fashion in the late 19th century. The 2nd Baron divided his time between Nostell, his London house in Grosvenor Square, and the south of France, where he liked to play golf for several months each year. He was a keen sportsman and spent part of the winter season shooting in Scotland. According to an article in *The World* in 1902, he travelled to the interior of Africa to hunt big game, where 'hippopotami and crocodile were to be numbered by the hundred'. His trophies once adorned the walls of the Lower Hall.

THE 20TH CENTURY

In 1914 the 2nd Baron organised a large gathering at Nostell of family, friends, employees, tenants and colliers to celebrate the coming-of-age of his eldest son, the Hon. Rowland Winn. Over 600 people gathered in a large marquee in the stable courtyard to witness the presentation of gifts and congratu-latory speeches. The festivities marked the end of an era at Nostell. Rowland, who became the 3rd Baron in 1919, did not live at Nostell after his father's death.

During the 1920s and '30s, the house was occupied periodically by the 2nd Baron's younger children, Charles, Reginald and Edith. Charles Winn and his family stayed most often, particularly during the shooting and racing seasons, when they entertained large parties of friends in the house. Charles kept a private plane at Nostell, using the great avenue to the east of the house as a runway. When the Winns were not in residence, the house was run by the permanent staff, including Mr Walker, the Butler, and Mrs Moore, the Housekeeper, a cook, footman, a kitchen- and housemaid, a pantry boy, odd-job man, dairyman and gardeners. During the Second World War,

Jane Waddington taking paint samples from the Library ceiling during the restoration work in 2000

Nostell was requisitioned by the Royal Artillery as a training base for new recruits. The grand rooms in the house were packed up, the stable block and servants' bedrooms were used as barracks, and the Lower Hall became a social room.

The 3rd Baron's eldest son, Rowland, 4th Baron St Oswald, returned to Nostell after the war, during which he had been awarded the Military Cross. He later served as Joint-Parliamentary

Charles Winn's aeroplane on the front lawn in the 1930s

Secretary to the Ministry of Agriculture and as a Member of the European Parliament. It was through his generosity, and that of the Trustees of the Nostell Estate, that the house was conveyed to the National Trust in lieu of tax in 1954. Following the death of the 4th Baron in 1984, the 5th Lord St Oswald and the Winn family, together with their advisers, arranged for the Chippendale furniture and some of the principal contents of the

house to be transferred to the Trust, and created a new Trust fund for the future care of the house. These actions ensured that the house and its treasures would be preserved for the enjoyment of future generations. The 5th Baron also managed the house and opened it to visitors until 1997, when the National Trust took on this responsibility. Nostell Priory is still the home of the present Lord and Lady St Oswald.

BIBLIOGRAPHY

PRIMARY SOURCES

The Nostell papers are on deposit in the Leeds District Archives, Chapeltown Road, Sheepscar, Leeds.

CONTEMPORARY SOURCES

ANON., 'A Series of Picturesque Views of Castles and Country Houses in Yorkshire' reprinted from the *Bradford Illustrated Weekly Telegraph*, Bradford, 1885.

ANON., 'Celebrities at Home: Lord St Oswald at Nostell Priory, Yorkshire', *The World*, 14 May 1902, pp. 8–9.

CAPPE, Catharine, *Memoirs of the late Mrs Catharine Cappe*, 1820, pp. 80–103.

DIBDIN, T. F., *A Bibliographical, Antiquarian & Picturesque Tour in the Northern Counties of England and Scotland*, i, 1838.

WRIGHT, T. G., 'Reminiscences of Nostell', 1887, MS 803, Yorkshire Archaeological Society, Leeds.

SECONDARY SOURCES

ANON., 'Nostell Priory, Yorkshire. A Seat of Lord St Oswald', *Country Life*, 27 April 1907, pp. 594–602.

BOLTON, Arthur T., 'Nostell Priory, Yorkshire. A Seat of Lord St Oswald', *Country Life*, 31 October 1914, pp. 583–9.

BOYNTON, Lindsay, and GOODISON, Nicholas, 'Thomas Chippendale at Nostell Priory', *Furniture History*, iv, 1968, pp. 10–61 [publishes the accounts verbatim].

BOYNTON, Lindsay, and GOODISON, Nicholas, 'The Furniture of Thomas Chippendale at Nostell Priory', *Burlington Magazine*, May, June 1969, pp. 281–5, 351–60.

BROCKWELL, Maurice W., *Catalogue of the Pictures and Other Works of Art in the Collection of Lord St Oswald at Nostell Priory*, 1915.

BURROWS, T., 'The Foundation of Nostell Priory', *Yorkshire Archaeological Journal*, liii, 1981, pp. 31–5.

CARR-WHITWORTH, Roger, 'Furniture Conservation at Nostell Priory', *Country Life*, 29 April 1993, pp. 71–3.

CORNFORTH, John, 'Restoration at Nostell Priory', *Country Life*, 11 April 1985, pp. 946–51 [fire].

CORNFORTH, John, 'The Nostell Priory Doll's House', *Country Life*, 28 November 1985, pp. 1692–7.

GILBERT, Christopher, *The Life and Work of Thomas Chippendale*, London, 1978 [publishes the accounts verbatim].

GILBERT, Christopher, 'New Light on the Furnishings of Nostell Priory', *Furniture History*, 1990, pp. 53–66.

HUSSEY, Christopher, 'Nostell Priory', *Country Life*, cxi, 16, 23, 30 May 1952, pp. 1492, 1572, 1652.

JACKSON-STOPS, Gervase, 'Pre-Adam Furniture Designs at Nostell Priory', *Furniture History*, x, 1974, pp. 24–37.

LAING, Alastair, 'Sir Rowland and Lady Winn: A Conversation Piece at Nostell Priory', *Apollo*, April 2000, pp. 14–18.

LEACH, Peter, *James Paine*, London, 1988.

PAGE, W., 'The Priory of Nostell', *The History of the County of Yorkshire*, iii, 1974, pp. 231–5.

RAIKES, Sophie, '"A cultivated eye for the antique": Charles Winn and the enrichment of Nostell Priory in the nineteenth century', *Apollo*, April 2003, pp. 3–8.

ROBINSON, John Martin, 'R. J. Wyatt's "Flora and Zephyr" at Nostell', *The National Trust Year-book 1977–8*, 1978, pp. 30–34.

SYMONDS, R. W., 'Pre-Chippendale Furniture at Nostell Priory', *Country Life*, cxi, 25 April 1952, p. 1248.

WORSLEY, Giles, 'Thornton Hall, Lincolnshire', *Country Life*, 2 January 1986, pp. 18–21.